WHAT'S COOKING
wok & stir-fry

Siân Davies

WHITECAP BOOKS

D0875029

Produced by Haldane Mason, London

Acknowledgments
Art Director: Ron Samuels
Editorial Director: Sydney Francis
Editorial Consultant: Christopher Fagg
Managing Editor: Jo-Anne Cox
Design: Digital Artworks Partnership Ltd
Photography: Iain Bagwell
Home Economists: Emma Patmore and Penny Stephens
Home Economists' Assistants: Nicky Deeley and Jane Stephens

Note
Unless otherwise stated,
milk is assumed to be full-fat, eggs are medium,
and pepper is freshly ground black pepper.

Contents

Introduction

Asian cookery basically requires the use of a wok. If you have one, then a whole array of wonderful dishes is open to you. It is worth buying a wok, rather than using a skillet, for more satisfactory results when trying the delicious range of recipes which follow in this book.

Basically, a wok is a curved, shallow, bowl-like cooking implement which is made of metal and has either a single long, wooden handle or two looped handles at opposite sides of the pan. It comes in many sizes, but the most appropriate for a family is approximately 12–14 inches in diameter. It may be made from a variety of different materials, including stainless steel, cast iron, or copper, the cast iron being the best choice as it retains heat more efficiently, especially when well seasoned. There are numerous advantages to a wok over a skillet. The convex shape means that food is easily moved around the wok and tossed (the basis of stir-frying) and cooks much more quickly. It can easily be tilted if required or rotated to reach ingredients easily.

Owing to the curved sides of the wok, the heat rises and the whole wok becomes a hot cooking surface. It therefore conserves fuel and is perfect for quick cooking and stir-frying. Cleaning is no problem, as there are no corners or edges in which food can become lodged.

USEFUL EQUIPMENT

There are several other pieces of equipment that will be useful with a wok. One of the most important in the Western kitchen is a **collar**. Basically this is a metal crown with angled sides and hollows which aids heat convection from our modern hobs and cooking rings. The wok sits in the collar and gives more even cooking than if the wok were simply placed on an electric ring. A **long-handled spatula** is useful for removing and cooking foods, as the curved edge follows the curve of the wok. Be sure to buy one with a wooden handle to insulate your hands from the heat.

The wok is mainly used for stir-frying, but may also be used for deep-frying and steaming. A **frying strainer** or **shallow wire-meshed basket** is useful to remove foods from fat and a **steaming trivet** will convert your wok to a steamer.

Obviously, a **lid** is essential for some wok cooking and should be domed and fit snugly inside the wok to seal in the flavors during steaming. Many boxed wok sets contain all of these additional pieces of equipment, as they are an essential part of wok cooking if it is to be used to its full potential.

USING YOUR WOK

Before using your wok it is essential to season it, as with other pans. Wipe the wok inside and out with oiled paper towels and heat it to a high heat in the oven or on the hob. Remove the wok from the heat, allow it to cool, and repeat this process several times to give a good coating—this will make it easier to clean and give it a nonstick coating. After the initial seasoning, the wok may be cleaned with soap and water, but it must be dried immediately if made of cast iron, to prevent it from rusting. Generally, the wok is simply wiped clean, and allowed to blacken with use. It is said that the blacker the wok, the better the cook, as it shows how frequently the wok is used.

STIR-FRYING

The wok is most widely used for stir-frying, a cooking method which originated in China, and remains the most recognized form of Chinese cooking. This method has spread throughout East Asia. In China it is called *Ch'au*, which primarily means one or a number of ingredients are sliced thinly and evenly and cooked in 1–2 tablespoons of fat. The food is stirred with long bamboo chopsticks or a spatula and seasonings and sauces may be added.

Stir-frying is often done in stages. This allows foods which have longer cooking times to be stir-fried and removed, and then returned to the wok at a later stage, and also for individual flavors to be kept distinct. The dish is always brought together at the end of cooking in the wok and served as a whole. Usually peanut or corn oil are used to fry the foods, but occasionally chicken fat and sometimes lard will be used for more delicate flavors.

There are different types of stir-frying which are described below:

Liu is wet frying with less vigorous stirring and more turning of the foods. A cornstarch and stock mixture is added with sugar, vinegar, and soy sauce at the end of cooking for a delicious coating sauce.

Pao, or "explosion," requires foods to be fried at the highest heat, and it is a very short, sharp method of cooking, usually lasting only 1 minute. Foods cooked in this way are generally marinated beforehand for flavor and tenderness.

WOK COOKING AROUND THE WORLD

Across the Far East woks are used in various guises for many dishes. In India, a large pan or *karahi* is used which sits over a hole in a brick or earth oven.

This wok-like vessel is used for braising and frying, the infamous curry or *karahi* deriving its name from the pan. In Indonesia, a *wajan* or wok is used over wood or charcoal for curries, rice dishes, and quick stir-fries—the same applies in Japan, Thailand, Singapore, and Malaysia, all of which have been influenced by Chinese cooking. Even a Mongolian barbecue resembles a wok, being a convex iron griddle.

You will gather from the preceding information, that the wok and the stir-frying cooking method are both essential and unique to Asian and Far Eastern cooking, being swift, light, healthy, and extremely versatile. The following recipes take you on a magical journey of the Far East, covering soups, starters, meat and poultry, fabulous fish dishes, vegetarian dishes, and, of course, rice and noodles, the staples in these countries. So get out your wok and prepare yourself for the feast of flavors now open to you!

Soups & Starters

Soup is indispensable at Asian tables, especially in China, Japan, Korea, and Southeast Asia. Chicken soup, for example, is sometimes served in China, Malaysia, and Thailand for breakfast! However, it is generally eaten part way through a main meal to clear the palate for further dishes, but it is never served as a starter as in the Western world. There are many different types of delicious soups, both thick and thin, and, of course, the clear soups which are often served with wontons or dumplings in them. In Japan, the clear soups are exquisite arrangements of fish, meat, and vegetables in a clear broth.

Starters or snacks are drier foods in general, such as spring rolls, which come in many variations and shapes across the Far East. Satay is served in Indonesia, Malaysia, and Thailand and other delights are wrapped in pastry, bread, or rice paper or skewered for ease of eating. Again, these are generally served as snacks in their native countries, but are frequent starters in Westernized restaurants.

The following chapter contains many delicious recipes for both soups and starters, all of which are the perfect way to begin a meal and whet the appetite for the delicious dishes that follow.

Spicy Chicken Noodle Soup

*This filling soup is packed with Thai flavors and color
for a really attractive and hearty dish.*

Serves 4

INGREDIENTS

2 tbsp tamarind paste

4 red Thai chilies, finely chopped

2 cloves garlic, crushed

1-inch piece Thai ginger, peeled and
very finely chopped

4 tbsp fish sauce

2 tbsp palm sugar or brown sugar

8 lime leaves, roughly torn

5 cups chicken stock

12 ounces boneless chicken breast

1–2 medium carrots, very thinly
sliced

12 ounces sweet potato, diced

3^1/$_2$ ounces baby corn cobs, halved

3 tbsp fresh cilantro, roughly
chopped

3^1/$_2$ ounces cherry tomatoes, halved

5^1/$_2$ ounces flat rice noodles

fresh cilantro, chopped,
to garnish

1 Place the tamarind paste,
Thai chilies, garlic, Thai
ginger, fish sauce, sugar, lime
leaves, and chicken stock in a
large preheated wok and bring
to a boil, stirring constantly.
Reduce the heat and cook for
about 5 minutes.

2 Using a sharp knife, thinly
slice the chicken. Add the
chicken to the wok and cook for
a further 5 minutes, stirring the
mixture well.

3 Reduce the heat slightly and
add the carrots, sweet potato,
and baby corn cobs to the wok.
Simmer, uncovered, for about
5 minutes, or until the vegetables
are just tender and the chicken is
completely cooked through.

4 Stir in the cilantro, cherry
tomatoes and noodles.
Simmer for about 5 minutes, or
until the noodles are tender.
Transfer to warm bowls, garnish
and serve hot.

COOK'S TIP

*Tamarind paste is produced from
the seed pod of the tamarind tree. It
adds both a brown color and tang to
soups and gravies. If unavailable,
dilute brown sugar or molasses
with lime juice.*

Crab & Corn Noodle Soup

Crab and corn are classic ingredients in Chinese cookery. Here egg noodles are added for a filling dish.

Serves 4

INGREDIENTS

1 tbsp sunflower oil
1 tsp Chinese five-spice powder
3–4 medium carrots, cut into sticks
$1/2$ cup canned or frozen corn
$3/4$ cup peas

6 scallions, trimmed and sliced
1 red chili, seeded and very
  thinly sliced
2 x 7 ounce can white crab meat
6 ounces egg noodles

$7^{1}/2$ cups fish stock
3 tbsp soy sauce

1 Heat the sunflower oil in a large preheated wok.

2 Add the Chinese five-spice powder, carrots, corn, peas, scallions, and chili to the wok and stir fry for about 5 minutes.

3 Add the crab meat to the wok and stir-fry the mixture for 1 minute.

4 Roughly break up the egg noodles into smaller pieces and add to the wok.

5 Pour the stock and soy sauce into the mixture in the wok, bring to a boil, cover, and simmer for 5 minutes.

6 Transfer the soup to warm serving bowls and serve at once.

COOK'S TIP

Chinese five-spice powder is a mixture of star anise, fennel, cloves, cinnamon, and Szechuan pepper.

COOK'S TIP

Use thin egg noodles for the best result in this recipe.

Spicy Thai Soup with Shrimp

Lime is a classic flavoring in Thai cooking
which adds tartness to this soup.

Serves 4

INGREDIENTS

2 tbsp tamarind paste
4 red Thai chilies, very finely chopped
2 cloves garlic, crushed
1 inch piece Thai ginger, peeled and
  very finely chopped
4 tbsp fish sauce
2 tbsp palm sugar or brown sugar

8 lime leaves, roughly torn
5 cups fish stock
1–2 medium carrots, very
  thinly sliced
12 ounces sweet potato, diced
1 cup baby corn cobs, halved

3 tbsp fresh cilantro, roughly
  chopped
3½ ounces cherry tomatoes, halved
8 ounces fan-tail shrimp

1 Place the tamarind paste, Thai chilies, garlic, ginger, fish sauce, palm or brown sugar, lime leaves, and fish stock in a large preheated wok. Bring to a boil, stirring constantly.

2 Reduce the heat and add the carrot, sweet potato, and baby corn to the mixture in the wok.

3 Simmer the soup, uncovered, for about 10 minutes, or until the vegetables are just tender.

4 Stir the cilantro, cherry tomatoes, and shrimp into the soup and heat through for about 5 minutes.

5 Transfer the soup to warm serving bowls and serve hot.

COOK'S TIP

Palm sugar is a thick, coarse brown sugar that has a slightly caramel taste. It is sold in round cakes.

COOK'S TIP

Thai ginger or galangal is a member of the ginger family, but it is yellow in color with pink sprouts. The flavor is aromatic and less pungent than ginger.

Coconut & Crab Soup

Thai red curry paste is quite fiery, but adds a superb flavor to this dish.
It is available in jars or packets from supermarkets.

Serves 4

INGREDIENTS

1 tbsp peanut oil
2 tbsp Thai red curry paste
1 red bell pepper, seeded and sliced
2¹/₂ cups coconut milk

2¹/₂ cups fish stock
2 tbsp fish sauce
8 ounces canned or fresh white
  crab meat

8 ounces fresh or frozen crab claws
2 tbsp chopped fresh cilantro
3 scallions, trimmed and sliced

1 Heat the oil in a large preheated wok.

2 Add the red curry paste and red bell pepper to the wok and stir-fry for 1 minute.

3 Add the coconut milk, fish stock, and fish sauce to the wok and bring to a boil.

4 Add the crab meat (drained if canned), crab claws (thawed if frozen), cilantro, and scallions to the wok. Stir the mixture well and heat thoroughly for 2–3 minutes.

5 Transfer the soup to warm bowls and serve hot.

COOK'S TIP

Clean the wok after each use by washing it with water, using a mild detergent if necessary, and a soft cloth or brush. Do not scrub or use any abrasive cleaner, as this will scratch the surface. Dry thoroughly with paper towels or over a low heat, then wipe the surface all over with a little oil. This forms a sealing layer to protect the surface of the wok from moisture and prevents it rusting.

COOK'S TIP

Coconut milk adds a sweet and creamy flavor to the dish. It is available in powdered form or in cans ready to use.

Chili Fish Soup

Chinese mushrooms add an intense flavor to this soup that is unique.
Try to obtain them if you can, otherwise use open-cap mushrooms, sliced.

Serves 4

INGREDIENTS

$^{1}/_{2}$ ounce Chinese dried mushrooms
2 tbsp sunflower oil
1 onion, sliced
$1^{1}/_{2}$ cups snow peas

$1^{1}/_{2}$ cups bamboo shoots
3 tbsp sweet chili sauce
5 cups fish or vegetable stock
3 tbsp light soy sauce

2 tbsp fresh cilantro
1 pound cod fillet, skinned and cubed

1 Place the mushrooms in a large bowl. Pour over enough boiling water to cover and let stand for 5 minutes. Drain the mushrooms thoroughly. Using a sharp knife, remove the stalks and roughly chop the caps.

2 Heat the sunflower oil in a preheated wok. Add the onion to the wok and stir-fry for 5 minutes, or until softened.

3 Add the snow peas, bamboo shoots, chili sauce, stock, and soy sauce to the wok and bring to a boil.

4 Add the cilantro and cubed fish to the wok. Lower the heat slightly and simmer for about 5 minutes, or until the fish is cooked through.

5 Transfer the soup to warm bowls, garnish with extra cilantro, if wished, and serve hot.

COOK'S TIP

There are many different varieties of dried mushrooms, but shiitake are best. They are not cheap, but a small quantity will go a long way.

VARIATION

Cod is used in this recipe, as it is a meaty white fish. For real luxury, use monkfish tail instead.

Hot & Sour Mushroom Soup

Hot and sour soups are found across Southeast Asia in different forms. Take care with the chilies and reduce the number added if you prefer a milder dish.

Serves 4

INGREDIENTS

2 tbsp tamarind paste
4 red Thai chilies, very finely chopped
2 cloves garlic, crushed
1-inch piece of Thai ginger, peeled and very finely chopped
4 tbsp fish sauce
2 tbsp palm sugar or brown sugar

8 lime leaves, roughly torn
5 cups vegetable stock
1–2 medium carrots, very thinly sliced
3¼ cups button mushrooms, halved
12 ounces shredded white cabbage
¾ cup fine green beans, halved

3 tbsp fresh cilantro, roughly chopped
3½ ounces cherry tomatoes, halved

1 Place the tamarind paste, Thai chilies, garlic, Thai ginger, fish sauce, palm or brown sugar, lime leaves, and stock in a large preheated wok. Bring the mixture to a boil, stirring occasionally.

2 Reduce the heat slightly and add the carrots, mushrooms, cabbage, and green beans. Simmer the soup, uncovered, for about 10 minutes, or until the vegetables are just tender.

3 Stir the cilantro and cherry tomatoes into the mixture in the wok and heat through for 5 minutes.

4 Transfer the soup to warm bowls and serve hot.

COOK'S TIP

Tamarind is one of the ingredients that gives Thai cuisine its special sweet and sour flavor.

VARIATION

Instead of the white cabbage, try using Chinese cabbage for a sweeter flavor. Add the Chinese cabbage with the cilantro and cherry tomatoes in step 3.

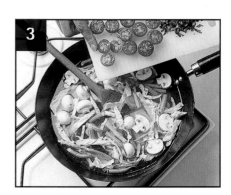

Thai-Style Spicy Corn Fritters

Cornmeal can be found in most supermarkets or health-food shops.
It is yellow in color, it acts as a binding agent in this recipe.

Serves 4

INGREDIENTS

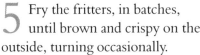

1 $\frac{1}{3}$ cup canned or frozen corn
2 red Thai chilies, seeded and very
    finely chopped
2 cloves garlic, crushed

10 lime leaves, very finely chopped
2 tbsp fresh cilantro, chopped
1 large egg
$\frac{1}{2}$ cup cornmeal

$\frac{3}{4}$ cup fine green beans, very
    finely sliced
peanut oil, for frying

1 Place the corn, chilies, garlic, lime leaves, cilantro, egg, and cornmeal in a large mixing bowl, and stir to combine.

2 Add the green beans to the ingredients in the bowl and mix well, using a wooden spoon.

3 Divide the cornmeal mixture into small, even-size balls. Flatten the balls of mixture between the palms of your hands to form rounds.

4 Heat a little peanut oil in a preheated wok.

5 Fry the fritters, in batches, until brown and crispy on the outside, turning occasionally.

6 Transfer the corn fritters to warm serving plates and serve immediately.

COOK'S TIP

Kaffir lime leaves are dark green, glossy leaves that have a lemony-lime flavor. They can be bought from specialty Asian stores either fresh or dried. Fresh leaves impart the most delicious flavor.

COOK'S TIP

If using canned corn, drain thoroughly and then rinse, and drain thoroughly again before use.

Vegetable Spring Rolls

There are many different versions of spring rolls throughout the Far East,
a vegetable filling being the classic.

Serves 4

INGREDIENTS

3–4 medium carrots
1 red bell pepper
1 tbsp sunflower oil, plus extra
　for frying
1/3 cup bean sprouts
finely grated zest and juice of 1 lime

1 red chili, seeded and very
　finely chopped
1 tbsp soy sauce
1/2 tsp arrowroot
2 tbsp chopped fresh cilantro
8 sheets filo pastry

2 tbsp butter
2 tsp sesame oil
scallion tassels, to garnish
chili sauce, to serve

1 Using a sharp knife, cut the carrots into thin sticks. Seed the bell pepper and cut the flesh into thin slices.

2 Heat the sunflower oil in a large preheated wok.

3 Add the carrot, red bell pepper, and bean sprouts and cook, stirring, for 2 minutes, or until softened. Remove the wok from the heat and toss in the lime zest and juice, and the red chili.

4 Mix the soy sauce with the arrowroot. Stir the mixture into the wok, return to the heat, and cook for 2 minutes, or until the juices thicken. Add the cilantro and mix well.

5 Lay the sheets of filo pastry out on a board. Melt the butter with the sesame oil and brush each sheet with the mixture. Spoon a little of the vegetable filling at the top of each sheet, fold over each long side, and roll up.

6 Add a little oil to the wok and cook the spring rolls, in batches, for 2–3 minutes, or until crisp and golden. Garnish with scallion tassels and serve hot with chili dipping sauce.

COOK'S TIP

Use prepared spring roll skins
available from Chinese
supermarkets or healthfood shops
instead of the filo pastry if desired.

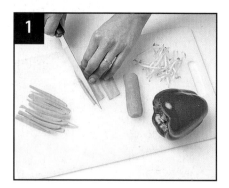

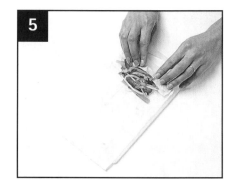

Seven-spice Eggplants

*This is a really simple dish which is perfect
served with a chili dip.*

Serves 4

INGREDIENTS

1 pound eggplants, wiped 1 egg white	7 tbsp cornstarch 1 tsp salt	1 tbsp Thai seven-spice seasoning oil, for deep-frying

1 Using a sharp knife, slice the eggplants into fairly thin rounds.

2 Place the egg white in a small bowl and beat until light and foamy.

3 Mix together the cornstarch, salt, and seven-spice powder on a large plate.

4 Heat the oil for deep-frying in a large wok.

5 Dip each piece of eggplant into the beaten egg white, then coat in the cornstarch and seven-spice mixture.

6 Deep-fry the coated eggplant slices, in batches, for about 5 minutes, or until pale golden brown and crispy.

7 Transfer the eggplants to absorbent paper towels to drain thoroughly. Transfer the slices to serving plates and serve hot.

COOK'S TIP

The best oil to use for deep-frying is peanut oil which has a high smoke point and mild flavor, so it will neither burn or taint the food. About 2½ cups oil is sufficient.

COOK'S TIP

Thai seven-spice seasoning can be found on the spice shelves of most large supermarkets.

Stir-Fried Bean Curd with Peanut & Chili Sauce

Golden pieces of bean curd are served in a hot and creamy peanut sauce for a classic vegetarian starter.

Serves 4

INGREDIENTS

1 pound bean curd, cubed
oil, for frying

SAUCE:
6 tbsp crunchy peanut butter
1 tbsp sweet chili sauce

$2/3$ cup coconut milk
1 tbsp tomato paste
$1/4$ cup chopped salted peanuts

1 Pat away any moisture from the bean curd, using absorbent paper towels.

2 Heat the oil in a large wok until very hot. Cook the bean curd, in batches, for about 5 minutes, or until golden and crispy. Remove the bean curd with a slotted spoon, transfer to absorbent paper towels and set aside to drain.

3 To make the sauce, mix together the crunchy peanut butter, sweet chili sauce, coconut milk, tomato paste, and chopped peanuts in a bowl. Add a little boiling water if necessary to achieve a smooth consistency.

4 Transfer the crispy fried bean curd to serving plates and serve with the peanut and chili sauce.

COOK'S TIP

Cook the peanut and chili sauce in a saucepan over a gentle heat before serving, if desired.

COOK'S TIP

Make sure that all of the moisture has been absorbed from the bean curd before frying, otherwise it will not crispen.

Crispy Seaweed

This is a tasty Chinese starter or accompaniment which is not all that it seems. Bok choy is fried, salted, and tossed with pine nuts, seaweed being totally absent from the recipe!

Serves 4

INGREDIENTS

2¹/₄ pounds bok choy
peanut oil, for deep frying (about
  3³/₄ cups)

1 tsp salt
1 tbsp sugar

¹/₂ cup toasted pine nuts

1 Rinse the bok choy leaves under cold running water, then pat dry thoroughly with absorbent paper towels.

2 Roll each bok choy leaf up, then slice through thinly so that the leaves are finely shredded.

3 Heat the oil in a large wok. Add the shredded leaves and fry for about 30 seconds, or until they shrivel up and become crispy (you may need to do this in about 4 batches).

4 Remove the crispy seaweed from the wok with a slotted spoon and set aside to drain on absorbent paper towels.

5 Transfer the crispy seaweed to a large bowl and toss with the salt, sugar, and pine nuts. Serve immediately.

COOK'S TIP

As a time-saver, you can use a food processor to shred the bok choy finely. Make sure you use only the best leaves; sort through the bok choy and discard any tough, outer leaves, as these will spoil the overall taste and texture of the dish.

VARIATION

Use Savoy cabbage instead of the bok choy if it is unavailable, making sure the leaves are well dried before frying.

Spicy Chicken Livers with Bok Choy

This is a richly flavored dish with a dark, slightly tangy sauce which is popular in China.

Serves 4

INGREDIENTS

12 ounces chicken livers
2 tbsp sunflower oil
1 red chili, seeded and finely chopped
1 tsp fresh grated ginger

2 cloves garlic, crushed
2 tbsp tomato ketchup
3 tbsp sherry
3 tbsp soy sauce

1 tsp cornstarch
1 pound bok choy
egg noodles, to serve

1 Using a sharp knife, trim the fat from the chicken livers and slice them into small pieces.

2 Heat the oil in a large preheated wok. Add the chicken liver pieces and stir-fry over a high heat for 2–3 minutes.

3 Add the chili, ginger, and garlic and stir-fry for about 1 minute.

4 Mix together the tomato ketchup, sherry, soy sauce, and cornstarch in a small bowl and set aside.

5 Add the bok choy to the wok and stir-fry until it just wilts.

6 Add the reserved tomato ketchup mixture to the wok and cook, stirring to mix, until the juices start to bubble.

7 Transfer to serving bowls and serve hot with noodles.

COOK'S TIP

Fresh ginger root will keep for several weeks in a dry, cool place.

COOK'S TIP

Chicken livers are available fresh or frozen from most supermarkets.

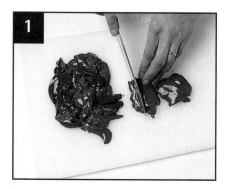

Thai-style Fish Cakes

*These small fish cakes are quick to make
and are delicious served with a chili dip.*

Serves 4

INGREDIENTS

1 pound cod fillets, skinned

2 tbsp fish sauce

2 red Thai chilies, seeded and very
    finely chopped

2 cloves garlic, crushed

10 lime leaves, very finely chopped

2 tbsp fresh cilantro, chopped

1 large egg

$^1/_4$ cup all-purpose flour

$^3/_4$ cup fine green beans, very
    finely sliced

peanut oil, for frying

1 Using a sharp knife, roughly cut the cod fillets into bite-size pieces.

2 Place the cod pieces in a food processor, together with the fish sauce, chilies, garlic, lime leaves, cilantro, egg and all-purpose flour. Process until finely chopped and turn out into a large mixing bowl.

3 Add the green beans to the cod mixture and combine.

4 Divide the mixture into small balls. Flatten the balls between the palms of your hands to form rounds.

5 Heat a little oil in a preheated wok. Fry the fish cakes on both sides until brown and crispy on the outside.

6 Transfer the fish cakes to serving plates and serve hot.

VARIATION

*Almost any kind of fish fillets and
seafood can used in this recipe, try
haddock, crab meat, or lobster.*

COOK'S TIP

*Fish sauce is a salty, brown liquid
which is a must for authentic flavor.
It is used to salt dishes, but is
milder in flavor than soy sauce. It is
available from Chinese foodstores or
healthfood shops.*

Crispy Chili & Peanut Shrimp

Peanut flavors are widely used in Far East and Southeast Asian cooking and complement many ingredients. Here, combined with fresh shrimp, they create a delicate and delicious dish.

Serves 4

INGREDIENTS

1 pound jumbo shrimp, peeled apart from the tails
3 tbsp crunchy peanut butter

1 tbsp chili sauce
10 sheets filo pastry
2 tbsp butter, melted

1³/₄ ounces fine egg noodles
oil, for frying

1 Using a sharp knife, make a small horizontal slit across the back of each shrimp. Press down on the shrimp so that they lie flat.

2 Mix together the peanut butter and chili sauce in a small bowl. Spread a little of the sauce onto each shrimp.

3 Cut each pastry sheet in half and brush one side of each sheet with melted butter.

4 Wrap each shrimp in a piece of pastry, tucking the edges under to enclose the shrimp fully.

5 Place the egg noodles in a bowl, pour over enough boiling water to cover, and let stand for 5 minutes. Drain the noodles thoroughly. Use 2–3 cooked noodles to tie around each shrimp.

6 Heat the oil in a preheated wok. Cook the shrimp for 3–4 minutes, or until golden and crispy.

7 Remove the shrimp with a slotted spoon, transfer to absorbent paper towels and set aside to drain. Transfer to serving plates and serve warm.

COOK'S TIP

When using filo pastry, keep any unused pastry covered to prevent it from drying out.

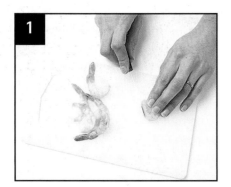

Shrimp Packets

These small shrimp bites are packed with the flavor of lime and cilantro for a quick and tasty starter.

Serves 4

INGREDIENTS

1 tbsp sunflower oil
1 red bell pepper, seeded and very
  thinly sliced
$1/3$ cup bean sprouts
finely grated zest and juice of 1 lime
1 red Thai chili, seeded and very
  finely chopped

$1/2$-inch piece of ginger root, peeled
  and grated
8 ounces peeled shrimp
1 tbsp fish sauce
$1/2$ tsp arrowroot
2 tbsp chopped fresh cilantro

8 sheets filo pastry
2 tbsp butter
2 tsp sesame oil
oil, for frying
scallion tassels, to garnish
chili sauce, to serve

1 Heat the sunflower oil in a large preheated wok. Add the red bell pepper and bean sprouts and stir-fry for 2 minutes, or until the vegetables have softened.

2 Remove the wok from the heat and toss in the lime zest and juice, red chili, ginger, and shrimp, stirring well.

3 Mix the fish sauce with the arrowroot and stir the mixture into the wok juices.

Return the wok to the heat and cook, stirring, for 2 minutes, or until the juices thicken. Toss in the cilantro and mix well.

4 Lay the sheets of filo pastry out on a board. Melt the butter with the sesame oil and brush the pastry with the mixture.

5 Spoon a little of the shrimp filling onto the top of each sheet, fold over each end, and roll up to enclose the filling.

6 Heat the oil in a large wok. Cook the packets, in batches, for 2–3 minutes, or until crisp and golden. Garnish with scallion tassels and serve hot with a chili dipping sauce.

COOK'S TIP

 If using cooked shrimp, cook for 1 minute only, otherwise the shrimp will toughen.

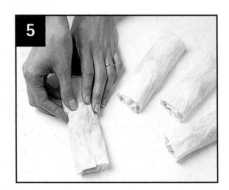

Chinese Shrimp Salad

Noodles and bean sprouts form the basis of this refreshing salad which combines the flavors of fruit and shrimp for a quick and delicious dish.

Serves 4

INGREDIENTS

9 ounces fine egg noodles	³/₄ cup bean sprouts	12 ounces peeled cooked shrimp
3 tbsp sunflower oil	1 ripe mango, sliced	2 tbsp light soy sauce
1 tbsp sesame oil	6 scallions, sliced	1 tbsp sherry
1 tbsp sesame seeds	2³/₄ ounces radishes, sliced	

1 Place the egg noodles in a large bowl and pour over enough boiling water to cover. Let stand for 10 minutes.

2 Drain the noodles thoroughly and pat away any moisture with absorbent paper towels.

3 Heat the sunflower oil in a large preheated wok. Add the noodles and stir-fry for 5 minutes, tossing frequently.

4 Remove the wok from the heat and add the sesame oil, sesame seeds, and bean sprouts, tossing to mix well.

5 In a separate bowl, mix together the sliced mango, scallions, radishes, shrimp, light soy sauce, and sherry.

6 Toss the shrimp mixture with the noodles or alternatively, arrange the noodles around the edge of a serving plate and pile the shrimp mixture into the center. Serve immediately.

VARIATION

If fresh mango is unavailable, use canned mango slices, rinsed and drained, instead.

Sesame Shrimp Toasts

These are one of the most recognized and popular starters in Chinese restaurants in the Western world. Quick and easy to make, they will soon feature on all your dinner-party menus.

Serves 4

INGREDIENTS

4 slices medium, thick-sliced
 white bread
8 ounces cooked peeled shrimp
1 tbsp soy sauce

2 cloves garlic, crushed
1 tbsp sesame oil
1 egg
2 tbsp sesame seeds

oil, for frying
sweet chili sauce, to serve

1 Remove the crusts from the bread, if desired, then set the slices of bread aside until they are required.

2 Place the peeled shrimp, soy sauce, crushed garlic, sesame oil, and egg in a food processor and process until a smooth paste has formed.

3 Spread the shrimp paste evenly over the 4 slices of bread.

4 Sprinkle the sesame seeds over the top of the shrimp mixture and press the seeds down with your hands so that they stick to the mixture.

5 Cut each slice of bread in half and then in half again to form 4 triangles.

6 Heat the oil in a large wok and deep-fry the toasts, sesame seed side up, for 4-5 minutes, or until golden and crispy.

7 Remove the toasts with a slotted spoon, transfer to absorbent paper towels and set aside to drain thoroughly. Serve the shrimp toasts warm with sweet chili sauce for dipping.

VARIATION

Add two chopped scallions to the mixture in step 2 for added flavor and crunch.

Shrimp Omelet

This is called Foo Yung *in China and is a classic dish which may be flavored with any ingredients you have to hand. It is a quick and delicious omelet.*

Serves 4

INGREDIENTS

3 tbsp sunflower oil
2 leeks, trimmed and sliced
12 ounces raw jumbo shrimp
4 tbsp cornstarch

1 tsp salt
2$^1/_3$ cups sliced mushrooms
$^3/_4$ cup bean sprouts

6 eggs
deep-fried leeks, to garnish (optional)

1 Heat the sunflower oil in a large preheated wok. Add the sliced leeks and stir-fry for about 3 minutes.

2 Rinse the shrimp under cold running water, drain, and then pat thoroughly dry with absorbent paper towels.

3 Mix together the cornstarch and salt in a large bowl.

4 Add the jumbo shrimp to the cornstarch and salt mixture and toss well to coat them all over.

5 Add the coated shrimp to the wok and stir-fry for 2 minutes, or until the shrimp are almost cooked through.

6 Add the mushrooms and bean sprouts to the wok and stir-fry for a further 2 minutes.

7 Lightly beat the eggs with 3 tablespoons of cold water. Pour the egg mixture into the wok and cook until the egg has just set, carefully turning the omelet over once. Turn the omelet out onto a clean board, divide it into 4 portions, and transfer to warm plates. Serve hot, garnished with deep-fried leeks (if using).

COOK'S TIP

If desired, divide the mixture into 4 once the initial cooking has taken place in step 6 and cook 4 individual omelets.

Salt & Pepper Shrimp

Szechuan peppercorns are very hot, adding heat and a red color to the shrimp.
They are effectively offset by the sugar in this recipe.

Serves 4

INGREDIENTS

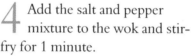

2 tsp salt
1 tsp black pepper
2 tsp Szechuan peppercorns
1 tsp sugar

1 pound peeled raw jumbo shrimp
2 tbsp peanut oil
1 red chili, seeded and finely chopped
1 tsp freshly grated ginger

3 cloves garlic, crushed
scallions, sliced, to garnish
shrimp crackers, to serve

1 Finely grind the salt, black pepper and Szechuan peppercorns in a mortar with a pestle. Mix the salt and pepper mixture with the sugar and set aside until required.

2 Rinse the shrimp under cold running water and pat dry with absorbent paper towels.

3 Heat the oil in a preheated wok. Add the shrimp, chili, ginger, and garlic and stir-fry for 4–5 minutes, or until the shrimp are cooked through and have changed color.

4 Add the salt and pepper mixture to the wok and stir-fry for 1 minute.

5 Transfer to warm serving bowls and garnish with sliced scallion. Serve immediately with shrimp crackers.

COOK'S TIP

Szechuan peppercorns are also known as farchiew. *These wild reddish-brown peppercorns from the Szechuan region of China add an aromatic flavor to a dish.*

COOK'S TIP

Jumbo shrimp are widely available and are not only colorful and tasty, but they have a meaty texture, too. If cooked jumbo shrimp are used, add them with the salt and pepper mixture in step 4—if the cooked shrimp are added any earlier they will toughen up and be inedible.

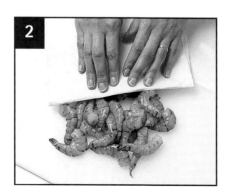

Meat & Poultry

Meat is expensive in Far Eastern countries and is eaten in smaller proportions than in the Western world. However, meat is used to its full potential—it is marinated or spiced and combined with other delicious native flavorings to create a wide array of delicious dishes.

In Malaysia, a wide variety of spicy meats is offered, reflecting the many ethnic origins of the population. Chicken is the most frequently used poultry in Malaysia—it is marinated and broiled, stir-fried, or cooked in the wok as delicious curries and stews.

In China, poultry, lamb, beef, and pork are stir-fried or steamed in the wok and combined with sauces and seasonings, such as soy, black bean and oyster sauce, and in Japan where a smaller amount of meat is consumed, it is generally marinated and quickly stir-fried in a wok or simmered in miso stock.

The use of meat in Thailand is similar, but it is leaner and has more flavor due to "free-range" rearing. Meats differ slightly in that beef is probably taken from the buffalo, and lamb on the menu can often turn out to be goat! There are no such demands in the following chapter, commonly available meats are perfectly acceptable.

Stir-Fried Ginger Chicken

The oranges add color and piquancy to this refreshing dish,
which complements the chicken well.

Serves 4

INGREDIENTS

2 tbsp sunflower oil
1 onion, sliced
6 ounces carrots, cut into thin sticks
1 clove garlic, crushed
12 ounces boneless skinless chicken
   breasts

2 tbsp ginger root, peeled and grated
1 tsp ground ginger
4 tbsp sweet sherry
1 tbsp tomato paste
1 tbsp sugar
1/2 cup orange juice

1 tsp cornstarch
1 orange, peeled and segmented
fresh snipped chives, to garnish

1 Heat the oil in a large preheated wok. Add the onion, carrots, and garlic and stir-fry over a high heat for 3 minutes, or until the vegetables begin to soften.

2 Using a sharp knife, slice the chicken into thin strips. Add the chicken to the wok, together with the ginger root and ground ginger. Stir-fry for a further 10 minutes, or until the chicken is well cooked through and golden in color.

3 Mix together the sherry, tomato paste, sugar, orange juice, and cornstarch to a smooth paste in a bowl. Stir the mixture into the wok and heat through until the mixture bubbles and the juices start to thicken.

4 Add the orange segments and carefully toss to mix.

5 Transfer the stir-fried chicken to warm serving bowls and garnish with freshly snipped chives. Serve immediately.

COOK'S TIP

Make sure that you do not continue cooking the dish once the orange segments have been added in step 4, otherwise they will break up.

Chicken, Collard Green, & Yellow Bean Stir-Fry

Yellow bean sauce is made from yellow soy beans and is available in most supermarkets.
Try to buy a chunky sauce rather than a smooth one for texture.

Serves 4

INGREDIENTS

2 tbsp sunflower oil
1 pound skinless, boneless
   chicken breasts
2 cloves garlic, crushed
1 green bell pepper

$1^1/_2$ cups snow peas
6 scallions, sliced, plus extra
   to garnish
8 ounces collard greens or
   cabbage, shredded

$5^3/_4$ ounce jar yellow bean sauce
3 tbsp roasted cashew nuts

1 Heat the sunflower oil in a large preheated wok.

2 Using a sharp knife, slice the chicken into thin strips.

3 Add the chicken to the wok, together with the garlic. Stir-fry for about 5 minutes, or until the chicken is sealed on all sides and beginning to turn golden.

4 Using a sharp knife, seed the green bell pepper and cut the flesh into thin strips.

5 Add the snow peas, scallions, green bell pepper strips, and collard greens or cabbage to the wok. Stir-fry for a further 5 minutes, or until the vegetables are just tender.

6 Stir in the yellow bean sauce and heat through for about 2 minutes, or until the mixture starts to bubble.

7 Generously scatter the stir-fry with the roasted cashew nuts.

8 Transfer the chicken, collard green, and yellow bean stir-fry to warm serving plates and garnish with extra scallions, if desired. Serve the stir-fry immediately.

COOK'S TIP

Do not add salted cashew nuts to this dish, otherwise, combined with the slightly salty sauce, the dish will be very salty indeed.

Chicken, Bell Pepper, & Orange Stir-Fry

Chicken thighs are inexpensive, meaty portions of the chicken which are readily available.
The meat is not as tender as the breast, but it is perfect for stir-frying.

Serves 4

INGREDIENTS

3 tbsp sunflower oil
12 ounces skinless, boneless chicken
  thighs, cut into thin strips
1 onion, sliced
1 clove garlic, crushed

1 red bell pepper, seeded and sliced
1^1/$_4$ cups snow peas
4 tbsp light soy sauce
4 tbsp sherry
1 tbsp tomato paste
finely grated rind and juice of 1 orange

1 tsp cornstarch
2 oranges
^{1}/$_2$ cup bean sprouts
cooked rice or noodles, to serve

1 Heat the sunflower oil in a large preheated wok.

2 Add the strips of chicken to the wok and stir-fry for 2–3 minutes, or until sealed on all sides.

3 Add the sliced onion, garlic, bell pepper and snow peas to the wok. Stir-fry the mixture for a further 5 minutes, or until the vegetables are just becoming tender and the chicken is completely cooked through and golden brown.

4 Mix together the soy sauce, sherry, tomato paste, orange rind and juice, and the cornstarch to a smooth paste.

5 Add the mixture to the wok and cook, stirring, until the juices start to thicken.

6 Using a sharp knife, peel and segment the oranges.

7 Add the orange segments and bean sprouts to the mixture in the wok and heat through for a further 2 minutes.

8 Transfer the stir-fry to serving plates and serve at once with cooked rice or noodles.

COOK'S TIP

Bean sprouts are sprouting mung beans and are a regular ingredient in Chinese cooking. They require very little cooking and may even be eaten raw, if desired.

Coconut Chicken Curry

Okra or lady's fingers are slightly bitter in flavor. The pineapple and coconut in this recipe offsets them in both color and flavor.

Serves 4

INGREDIENTS

2 tbsp sunflower oil or 2 tbsp ghee
1 pound boneless, skinless chicken
    thighs or breasts
1 cup okra
1 large onion, sliced
2 cloves garlic, crushed
3 tbsp mild curry paste
2$\frac{1}{4}$ cups chicken stock

1 tbsp fresh lemon juice
$\frac{1}{2}$ cup creamed coconut
1$\frac{1}{4}$ cups fresh or canned pineapple,
    cubes
$\frac{2}{3}$ cup thick, unsweetened yogurt
2 tbsp chopped fresh cilantro
freshly boiled rice, to serve

TO GARNISH:
lemon wedges
fresh cilantro sprigs

1 Heat the sunflower oil or ghee in a large preheated wok.

2 Using a sharp knife, cut the chicken into bite-size pieces. Add the chicken to the wok and cook, stirring frequently, until evenly browned.

3 Using a sharp knife, trim the okra.

4 Add the onion, garlic, and okra to the wok and cook for a further 2–3 minutes, stirring constantly.

5 Mix the curry paste with the chicken stock and lemon juice and pour the mixture into the wok. Bring to a boil, cover, and simmer for 30 minutes.

6 Coarsely grate the creamed coconut, stir it into the curry, and cook for about 5 minutes—the creamed coconut will help to thicken the juices.

7 Add the pineapple, yogurt, and cilantro and heat through for 2 minutes, stirring.

8 Garnish and serve hot with boiled rice.

COOK'S TIP

Score around the top of the okra with a knife before cooking to release the sticky glue-like substance which is bitter in taste.

Sweet & Sour Chicken with Mango

This is quite a sweet dish, as mango has a sweet, scented flavor.

Serves 4

INGREDIENTS

1 tbsp sunflower oil
6 skinless, boneless chicken thighs
1 ripe mango
2 cloves garlic, crushed

8 ounces leeks, shredded
$^1/_2$ cup bean sprouts
$^2/_3$ cup mango juice
1 tbsp white wine vinegar

2 tbsp clear honey
2 tbsp tomato ketchup
1 tsp cornstarch

1 Heat the sunflower oil in a large preheated wok.

2 Using a sharp knife, cut the chicken into bite-size cubes.

3 Add the chicken to the wok and stir-fry over a high heat for 10 minutes, tossing frequently, until the chicken is cooked through and golden in color.

4 Meanwhile, peel and slice the mango.

5 Add the garlic, leeks, mango, and bean sprouts to the wok and stir-fry for a further 2–3 minutes, or until softened.

6 Thoroughly mix together the mango juice, white wine vinegar, clear honey, and tomato ketchup with the cornstarch to make a smooth paste.

7 Pour the mango juice and cornstarch mixture into the wok and stir-fry for a further 2 minutes, or until the juices start to thicken.

8 Transfer to a warm serving dish and serve immediately.

COOK'S TIP

Mango juice is available in jars from most supermarkets and is quite thick and sweet. If unavailable, purée and strain a ripe mango and add a little water to make up the required quantity.

Chicken Stir-Fry with Cumin Seeds & Trio of Bell Peppers

Cumin seeds are more frequently associated with Indian cooking, but they are used in this Chinese recipe for their earthy flavor. You could use ¹/₂ teaspoon ground cumin instead.

Serves 4

INGREDIENTS

1 pound boneless, skinless
  chicken breasts
2 tbsp sunflower oil
1 clove garlic, crushed
1 tbsp cumin seeds
1 tbsp grated fresh ginger root

1 red chili, seeded and sliced
1 red bell pepper, seeded
  and sliced
1 green bell pepper, seeded
  and sliced
1 yellow bell pepper, seeded
  and sliced

¹/₂ cup bean sprouts
12 ounces bok choy or other greens
2 tbsp sweet chili sauce
3 tbsp light soy sauce
deep-fried crispy ginger, to garnish
  (see Cook's Tip)

1 Using a sharp knife, slice the chicken breasts into thin strips.

2 Heat the oil in a large preheated wok.

3 Add the chicken to the wok and stir-fry for 5 minutes.

4 Add the garlic, cumin seeds, ginger, and chili to the wok, stirring to mix.

5 Add all the bell peppers to the wok and stir-fry for a further 5 minutes.

6 Toss in the bean sprouts and bok choy, together with the sweet chili sauce and soy sauce and continue to cook until the bok choy leaves start to wilt.

7 Transfer to warm serving bowls and garnish with deep-fried ginger (see Cook's Tip).

COOK'S TIP

To make the deep-fried ginger garnish, peel and thinly slice a large piece of ginger root, using a sharp knife. Carefully lower the slices of ginger into a wok or small pan of hot oil and cook for about 30 seconds. Remove the deep-fried ginger with a slotted spoon, transfer to absorbent paper towels and drain thoroughly.

Stir-Fried Chicken with Lemon & Sesame Seeds

Sesame seeds have a strong flavor which adds nuttiness to recipes.
They are perfect for coating these thin chicken strips.

Serves 4

INGREDIENTS

4 boneless, skinless chicken breasts
1 egg white
2 tbsp sesame seeds
2 tbsp vegetable oil

1 onion, sliced
1 tbsp demerara sugar
finely grated zest and juice of
  1 lemon

3 tbsp lemon curd
7 ounce can water chestnuts
lemon zest, to garnish

1 Place the chicken breasts between 2 sheets of plastic wrap and pound with a rolling pin to flatten. Slice the chicken into thin strips.

2 Beat the egg white until it is light and foamy.

3 Dip the chicken strips into the egg white, then into the sesame seeds until coated evenly.

4 Heat the oil in a large preheated wok.

5 Add the onion to the wok and stir-fry for 2 minutes, or until just softened.

6 Add the sesame-coated chicken to the wok and continue stir-frying for 5 minutes, or until the chicken turns golden.

7 Mix together the sugar, lemon zest, lemon juice, and the lemon curd and add the mixture to the wok. Allow the lemon mixture to bubble slightly without stirring.

8 Drain the water chestnuts and slice them thinly, using a sharp knife. Add the water chestnuts to the wok and heat through for 2 minutes. Transfer to serving bowls, garnish with lemon zest, and serve hot.

COOK'S TIP

Water chestnuts are commonly added to Chinese recipes for their crunchy texture, as they do not have a great deal of flavor.

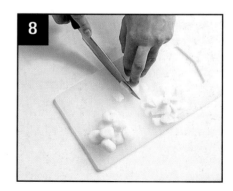

Thai Red Chicken with Cherry Tomatoes

This is a really colorful dish, the red of the tomatoes perfectly complementing the orange sweet potato.

Serves 4

INGREDIENTS

1 tbsp sunflower oil
1 pound boneless, skinless chicken
2 cloves garlic, crushed
2 tbsp Thai red curry paste
2 tbsp fresh grated galangal or
   ginger root

1 tbsp tamarind paste
4 lime leaves
8 ounces sweet potato
2¹/₂ cups coconut milk
8 ounces cherry tomatoes, halved

3 tbsp chopped fresh cilantro
cooked jasmine or Thai fragrant rice,
   to serve

1 Heat the sunflower oil in a large preheated wok.

2 Thinly slice the chicken. Add the chicken to the wok and stir-fry for 5 minutes.

3 Add the garlic, curry paste, galangal or ginger root, tamarind, and lime leaves to the wok and stir-fry for 1 minute.

4 Using a sharp knife, peel and dice the sweet potato.

5 Add the coconut milk and sweet potato to the mixture in the wok and bring to a boil. Allow to bubble over a medium heat for 20 minutes, or until the juices start to thicken and reduce.

6 Add the cherry tomatoes and cilantro to the curry and cook for a further 5 minutes, stirring occasionally. Transfer to warm serving plates and serve hot with cooked jasmine or Thai fragrant rice.

COOK'S TIP

Galangal is a spice very similar to ginger and is used to replace the latter in Thai cuisine. It can be bought fresh from Chinese foodstores, but is also available dried and as a powder. The fresh root, which is not as pungent as ginger, needs to be peeled before use.

Peppered Chicken Stir-fried with Sugar Snap Peas

Crushed mixed peppercorns coat tender, thin strips of chicken which are cooked with green and red bell peppers for a really colorful dish.

Serves 4

INGREDIENTS

2 tbsp tomato ketchup
2 tbsp soy sauce
1 pound boneless, skinless
chicken breasts

2 tbsp crushed mixed peppercorns
2 tbsp sunflower oil
1 red bell pepper
1 green bell pepper

2^1/$_2$ cups sugar snap peas
2 tbsp oyster sauce

1 Mix the tomato ketchup with the soy sauce in a bowl.

2 Using a sharp knife, slice the chicken into thin strips. Toss the chicken in the tomato ketchup and soy sauce mixture.

3 Sprinkle the crushed peppercorns onto a plate. Dip the coated chicken in the peppercorns until evenly coated.

4 Heat the sunflower oil in a preheated wok.

5 Add the chicken to the wok and stir-fry for 5 minutes.

6 Seed and slice the red and green bell peppers.

7 Add the bell peppers to the wok, together with the sugar snap peas and stir-fry for a further 5 minutes.

8 Add the oyster sauce and allow to bubble for 2 minutes. Transfer to warm serving bowls and serve immediately.

VARIATION

You could use snow peas instead of sugar snap peas, if desired.

Honey & Soy Stir-Fried Chicken with Bean Sprouts

Clear honey is often added to Chinese recipes for sweetness.
It combines well with the saltiness of the soy sauce.

Serves 4

INGREDIENTS

2 tbsp clear honey
3 tbsp light soy sauce
1 tsp Chinese five-spice powder
1 tbsp sweet sherry

1 clove garlic, crushed
8 chicken thighs
1 tbsp sunflower oil
1 fresh red chili

1 cup baby corn cobs, halved
8 scallions, sliced
$^3/_4$ cup bean sprouts

1 Mix together the honey, soy sauce, Chinese five-spice powder, sherry, and garlic in a large bowl.

2 Using a sharp knife, make 3 slashes in the skin of each chicken thigh. Brush the honey and soy marinade over the chicken thighs, cover and set aside for at least 30 minutes.

3 Heat the oil in a large preheated wok.

4 Add the chicken to the wok and cook over a fairly high heat for 12–15 minutes, or until the chicken browns and the skin begins to crispen. Remove the chicken with a slotted spoon.

5 Using a sharp knife, seed and very finely chop the chili.

6 Add the chili, corn cobs, scallions, and bean sprouts to the wok and stir-fry for about 5 minutes.

7 Return the chicken to the wok and mix all the ingredients together until completely heated through.

8 Transfer to serving plates and serve immediately.

COOK'S TIP

Chinese five-spice powder can be found in most large supermarkets and is a blend of aromatic spices.

Stir-Fried Chicken with Cashew Nuts & Yellow Bean Sauce

Chicken and cashew nuts is a great classic combination, and this recipe is no exception. Flavored with yellow bean sauce, it is a quick and delicious dish.

Serves 4

INGREDIENTS

1 pound boneless chicken breasts
2 tbsp vegetable oil
1 red onion, sliced

$2^1/4$ cups sliced flat mushrooms
1 cup cashew nuts
$2^3/4$ ounce jar yellow bean sauce

fresh cilantro, to garnish
egg fried rice or plain boiled rice,
   to serve

1 Using a sharp knife, remove the excess skin from the chicken breasts, if desired. Cut the chicken into small, bite-size chunks.

2 Heat the vegetable oil in a preheated wok.

3 Add the chicken to the wok and stir-fry for 5 minutes.

4 Add the red onion and mushrooms to the wok and continue to stir-fry for a further 5 minutes.

5 Place the cashew nuts on a cookie sheet and toast under a preheated broiler until just browning—this brings out their flavor and aroma.

6 Toss the toasted cashew nuts into the wok, together with the yellow bean sauce. Allow the sauce to bubble for 2–3 minutes.

7 Transfer the stir-fry to warm serving bowls and garnish with fresh cilantro. Serve hot with egg fried rice or plain boiled rice, if you wish.

COOK'S TIP

Chicken thighs could be used instead of the chicken breasts for a more economical dish.

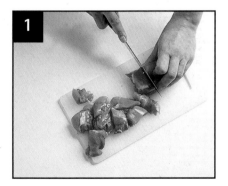

Stir-Fried Chicken with Chili & Crispy Basil

Chicken drumsticks are cooked in a delicious sauce and served with deep-fried basil for color and flavor.

Serves 4

INGREDIENTS

8 chicken drumsticks
2 tbsp soy sauce
1 tbsp sunflower oil
1 red chili

1–2 medium carrots, cut into thin sticks
6 celery stalks, cut into sticks
3 tbsp sweet chili sauce

oil, for frying
about 50 fresh basil leaves

1 Remove the skin from the chicken drumsticks, if desired. Make 3 slashes in each drumstick. Brush the drumsticks with the soy sauce.

2 Heat the oil in a preheated wok and fry the drumsticks for 20 minutes, turning frequently, until they are cooked through.

3 Seed and finely chop the chili. Add the chili, carrots, and celery to the wok and cook for

a further 5 minutes. Stir in the chili sauce, cover, and allow to bubble gently while preparing the basil leaves.

4 Heat a little oil in a heavy-based pan. Carefully add the basil leaves—stand well away from the pan and protect your hand with a dish cloth, as they may spit a little. Cook for about 30 seconds, or until they begin to curl up, but not brown. Transfer to paper towels to drain.

5 Transfer the cooked chicken, vegetables, and pan juices to to a warm serving plate and garnish with the deep-fried crispy basil leaves.

COOK'S TIP

Basil has a very strong flavor which is perfect with chicken and Chinese flavorings. You could use baby spinach instead of the basil, if desired.

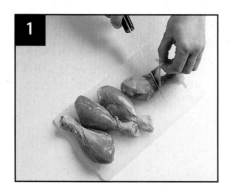

Stir-Fried Garlic Chicken with Cilantro & Lime

Garlic and cilantro butter flavors and moistens chicken breasts, which are served with a caramelized sauce, sharpened with lime juice.

Serves 4

INGREDIENTS

4 large skinless, boneless
chicken breasts
4 tbsp garlic butter, softened

3 tbsp chopped fresh cilantro
1 tbsp sunflower oil
finely grated zest and juice of 2 limes

4 tbsp palm sugar or brown sugar
boiled rice, to serve

1 Place each chicken breast between 2 sheets of plastic wrap and pound with a rolling pin until flattened to about ½ inch thick.

2 Mix together the garlic butter and cilantro and spread the mixture over each flattened chicken breast. Roll up like a jelly roll and secure with a toothpick.

3 Heat the oil in a wok. Add the chicken rolls and cook, turning frequently, for 15–20 minutes, or until cooked.

4 Remove the chicken from the wok and transfer to a board. Cut each chicken roll into slices.

5 Add the lime zest, juice, and sugar to the wok and heat gently, stirring, until the sugar has dissolved. Increase the heat and allow to bubble for 2 minutes.

6 Arrange the chicken on warm serving plates and spoon the pan juices over it to serve.

7 Garnish with extra fresh cilantro, if desired.

COOK'S TIP

Be sure to check that the chicken is cooked through before slicing and serving. Cook over a gentle heat to avoid overcooking the outside, while the inside remains raw.

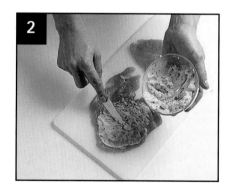
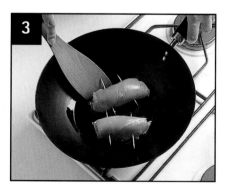

Stir-Fried Chicken with Cumin Seeds & Eggplant

This is a delicious curried chicken and eggplant dish, flavored with tomatoes and seasoned with fresh mint.

Serves 4

INGREDIENTS

5 tbsp sunflower oil
2 cloves garlic, crushed
1 tbsp cumin seeds
1 tbsp mild curry powder
1 tbsp paprika

1 pound boneless, skinless
    chicken breasts
1 large eggplant, cubed
4 tomatoes, cut into quarters
$1/2$ cup chicken stock

1 tbsp fresh lemon juice
$1/2$ tsp salt
$2/3$ cup unsweetened yogurt
1 tbsp chopped fresh mint

1 Heat 2 tablespoons of the sunflower oil in a large preheated wok.

2 Add the garlic, cumin seeds, curry powder, and paprika to the wok and stir-fry for 1 minute.

3 Using a sharp knife, thinly slice the chicken breasts.

4 Add the rest of the oil to the wok and stir-fry the chicken for 5 minutes.

5 Add the eggplant cubes, tomatoes, and chicken stock and bring to a boil. Reduce the heat slightly and simmer for about 20 minutes.

6 Stir in the lemon juice, salt, and yogurt and cook over a gentle heat for a further 5 minutes, stirring occasionally.

7 Scatter with chopped fresh mint and transfer to serving bowls. Serve immediately.

COOK'S TIP

Once the yogurt has been added, do not boil the sauce as the yogurt will curdle.

Hoisin Duck with Leek & Stir-Fried Cabbage

Duck is a strongly-flavored meat which benefits from the added citrus rind to counteract this rich taste.

Serves 4

INGREDIENTS

4 duck breasts
12 ounces green cabbage, outer
  leaves and stems removed

8 ounces leeks, sliced
finely grated zest of 1 orange
6 tbsp oyster sauce

1 tsp toasted sesame seeds, to serve

1 Heat a large wok and dry-fry the duck breasts, with the skin on, for 5 minutes on each side (you may need to do this in 2 batches).

2 Remove the duck breasts from the wok and transfer to a clean board. Using a sharp knife, cut the duck breasts into thin slices.

3 Remove all but 1 tablespoon of the fat from the duck left in the wok; discarding the rest.

4 Using a sharp knife, thinly shred the green cabbage.

5 Add the leeks, green cabbage, and orange zest to the wok and stir-fry for 5 minutes, or until the vegetables have softened.

6 Return the duck to the wok and heat through for 2–3 minutes.

7 Drizzle the oyster sauce over the top of the duck, toss well to combine, and then heat through.

8 Scatter with toasted sesame seeds and serve hot.

VARIATION

Use Chinese cabbage for a lighter, sweeter flavor instead of the green cabbage, if desired.

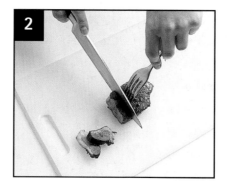

Duck with Baby Corn Cobs & Pineapple

*The pineapple and plum sauce adds a sweetness and fruity flavor
to this colorful recipe which blends well with the duck.*

Serves 4

INGREDIENTS

4 duck breasts
1 tsp Chinese five-spice powder
1 tbsp cornstarch
1 tbsp chili oil

8 ounces baby onions, peeled
2 cloves garlic, crushed
1 cup baby corn cobs
1¼ cups canned pineapple chunks

6 scallions, sliced
½ cup bean sprouts
2 tbsp plum sauce

1 Remove any skin from the duck breasts. Cut the duck breasts into thin slices.

2 Mix together the Chinese five-spice powder and the cornstarch in a large bowl.

3 Toss the duck in the five-spice powder and cornstarch mixture until well coated.

4 Heat the oil in a large preheated wok. Stir-fry the duck for about 10 minutes, or until just beginning to crispen around the edges.

5 Remove the duck from the wok and set aside until it is required.

6 Add the onions and garlic to the wok and stir-fry for 5 minutes, or until the onions have softened.

7 Add the baby corn cobs to the wok and stir-fry for a further 5 minutes.

8 Add the pineapple chunks, scallions, and bean sprouts and stir-fry for 3–4 minutes. Stir in the plum sauce.

9 Return the cooked duck to the wok and toss until well mixed. Transfer to warm serving dishes and serve hot.

COOK'S TIP

Buy pineapple chunks in natural juice rather than syrup for a fresher flavor. If you can obtain only pineapple in syrup, rinse it in cold water and drain thoroughly before using.

Stir-Fried Turkey with Cranberry Glaze

This dish encompasses all of the flavors of Thanksgiving with a Chinese theme! Turkey, cranberries, ginger, chestnuts, and soy sauce all blend perfectly in this quick stir-fry.

Serves 2–3

INGREDIENTS

1 turkey breast
2 tbsp sunflower oil
2 tbsp preserved ginger

$^1/_2$ cup fresh or frozen cranberries
$^1/_4$ cup canned chestnuts
4 tbsp cranberry sauce

3 tbsp light soy sauce
salt and pepper

1 Remove any skin from the turkey breast. Using a sharp knife, thinly slice the turkey breast.

2 Heat the oil in a large preheated wok.

3 Add the turkey to the wok and stir-fry for 5 minutes, or until cooked through.

4 Using a sharp knife, finely chop the preserved ginger.

5 Add the ginger and the cranberries to the wok and stir-fry for 2–3 minutes, or until the cranberries have softened.

6 Add the chestnuts, cranberry sauce, and soy sauce, season to taste with salt and pepper, and allow to bubble for 2–3 minutes.

7 Transfer to warm serving dishes and serve immediately.

COOK'S TIP

If you wish, use a turkey escalope instead of the breast for really tender, lean meat.

COOK'S TIP

It is very important that the wok is very hot before you stir-fry. This can be tested by holding your hand flat about 3 inches above the base of the interior—you should be able to feel the heat radiating from it.

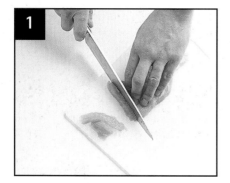

Stir-Fried Beef & Vegetables with Sherry & Soy Sauce

Fillet of beef is perfect for stir-frying, as it is so tender and lends itself to quick cooking.

Serves 4

INGREDIENTS

2 tbsp sunflower oil
12 ounces fillet of beef, sliced
1 red onion, sliced
8 ounces zucchini
5 medium carrots, thinly sliced
1 red bell pepper, seeded and sliced
1 small head Chinese cabbage,
  shredded

$^3/_4$ cup bean sprouts
8 ounce can bamboo shoots, drained
$^3/_4$ cup cashew nuts, toasted

SAUCE:
3 tbsp medium sherry
3 tbsp light soy sauce
1 tsp ground ginger

1 clove garlic, crushed
1 tsp cornstarch
1 tbsp tomato paste

1 Heat the sunflower oil in a large preheated wok.

2 Add the beef and onion to the wok and stir-fry for 4–5 minutes, or until the onion begins to soften and the meat is just browning.

3 Using a sharp knife, trim the zucchini and thinly slice diagonally.

4 Add the carrots, bell pepper, and zucchini, and stir-fry for 5 minutes.

5 Toss in the Chinese cabbage, bean sprouts, and bamboo shoots and heat through for 2–3 minutes, or until the cabbage is just beginning to wilt.

6 Scatter the cashews nuts over the stir-fry.

7 To make the sauce, mix together the sherry, soy sauce, ground ginger, garlic, cornstarch, and tomato paste. to make a smooth paste. Pour the sauce over the stir-fry and toss until well combined. Allow the sauce to bubble for 2–3 minutes, or until the juices start to thicken.

8 Transfer to warm serving dishes and serve at once.

Chili Beef Stir-Fry Salad

*This dish has a Mexican feel to it, combining
all of the classic flavors.*

Serves 4

INGREDIENTS

1 pound lean steak
2 cloves garlic, crushed
1 tsp chili powder
$\frac{1}{2}$ tsp salt
1 tsp ground coriander

1 ripe avocado
2 tbsp sunflower oil
15 ounce can red kidney
   beans, drained
6 ounces cherry tomatoes, halved

1 large packet tortilla chips
shredded iceberg lettuce
chopped fresh cilantro,
   to serve

1 Using a sharp knife, slice the steak into thin strips.

2 Place the garlic, chili powder, salt, and ground coriander in a large bowl and mix until thoroughly combined.

3 Add the strips of steak to the marinade and toss well to coat all over.

4 Using a sharp knife, peel the avocado. Slice the avocado lengthwise and then crosswise to form small dice.

5 Heat the oil in a large preheated wok. Add the steak and stir-fry, tossing frequently, for 5 minutes, until browned.

6 Add the kidney beans, tomatoes, and avocado and heat through for 2 minutes.

7 Arrange a bed of tortilla chips and iceberg lettuce around the edge of a large serving plate and spoon the steak mixture into the center. Alternatively, serve the steak and hand the tortilla chips and iceberg lettuce separately.

8 Garnish with chopped fresh cilantro and serve immediately.

COOK'S TIP

Serve this dish immediately, as avocado tends to discolor quickly. Once you have cut the avocado into dice, sprinkle it with a little lemon juice to prevent discoloration.

Marinated Beef Stir-Fry with Bamboo Shoots & Snow Peas

Tender beef, marinated in a soy and tomato sauce, is quickly stir-fried with crisp bamboo shoots and snow peas in this simple recipe.

Serves 4

INGREDIENTS

12 ounces steak

3 tbsp dark soy sauce

1 tbsp tomato ketchup

2 cloves garlic, crushed

1 tbsp fresh lemon juice

1 tsp ground coriander

2 tbsp vegetable oil

$2^3/4$ cups snow peas

7 ounce can bamboo shoots, drained

1 tsp sesame oil

1 Using a sharp knife, thinly slice the steak.

2 Place the meat in a nonmetallic dish, together with the dark soy sauce, tomato ketchup, garlic, lemon juice, and ground coriander. Mix well so that all of the steak is coated in the marinade, cover, and set aside for at least 1 hour.

3 Heat the vegetable oil in a preheated wok. Add the steak to the wok and stir-fry for 2–4 minutes, depending on how well cooked you like your meat, or until cooked through.

4 Add the snow peas and bamboo shoots to the mixture in the wok and stir-fry over a high heat, tossing frequently, for a further 5 minutes.

5 Drizzle with the sesame oil and toss well to combine.

6 Transfer to serving dishes and serve hot.

COOK'S TIP

Marinate the steak for at least 1 hour in order for the flavor to penetrate and increase the tenderness of the meat. If possible, marinate for a little longer for a fuller flavor to develop.

Stir-Fried Beef with Baby Onions & Palm Sugar

*Palm sugar or brown sugar is used in this recipe to give the beef
a slightly caramelized flavor.*

Serves 4

INGREDIENTS

1 pound beef fillet
2 tbsp soy sauce
1 tsp chili oil
1 tbsp tamarind paste

2 tbsp palm sugar or brown sugar
2 cloves garlic, crushed
2 tbsp sunflower oil
8 ounces baby onions

2 tbsp chopped fresh cilantro

1 Using a sharp knife, thinly slice the beef.

2 Place the slices of beef in a single layer in a large, shallow nonmetallic dish.

3 Mix together the soy sauce, chili oil, tamarind paste, sugar, and garlic.

4 Spoon the sugar mixture over the beef. Toss well to coat the beef in the mixture, cover, and set aside in the refrigerator to marinate for at least 1 hour.

5 Heat the sunflower oil in a preheated wok.

6 Peel the onions and cut them in half. Add the onions to the wok and stir-fry for 2–3 minutes, or until just browning.

7 Add the beef and marinade juices to the wok and stir-fry over a high heat for about 5 minutes.

8 Scatter with chopped fresh cilantro, transfer to a warm serving dish, and serve at once.

COOK'S TIP

Use the chili oil carefully as it is very hot and could easily spoil the dish if too much is added.

Sweet Potato Stir-Fry with Coconut Beef

This is a truly aromatic dish, blending the heat of red curry paste
with the aroma and flavor of the lime leaves and coconut.

Serves 4

INGREDIENTS

2 tbsp vegetable oil
12 ounces steak
2 cloves garlic
1 onion, sliced

12 ounces sweet potatoes
2 tbsp Thai red curry paste
1 1/4 cups coconut milk

3 limes leaves
cooked jasmine rice, to serve

1 Heat the vegetable oil in a large preheated wok.

2 Using a sharp knife, thinly slice the steak. Add the steak to the wok and stir-fry for about 2 minutes, or until sealed on all sides.

3 Add the garlic and the onion to the wok and stir-fry for a further 2 minutes.

4 Using a sharp knife, peel and dice the sweet potatoes.

5 Add the sweet potatoes to the wok with the curry paste, coconut milk and lime leaves and bring to a rapid boil. Reduce the heat, cover, and simmer for about 15 minutes, or until the sweet potatoes are tender.

6 Remove the lime leaves and transfer the stir-fry to warm serving bowls. Serve hot with cooked jasmine rice.

COOK'S TIP

There are two basic curry pastes used in Thai cuisine—red and green, depending on whether they are made from red or green chilies.

COOK'S TIP

If you cannot obtain lime leaves, use grated lime zest instead.

Beef with Green Peas & Black Bean Sauce

This recipe is the perfect example of quick stir-frying ingredients for a delicious, crisp, colorful dish.

Serves 4

INGREDIENTS

1 pound steak
2 tbsp sunflower oil
1 onion

2 cloves garlic, crushed
1 1/4 cup fresh or frozen peas
5 3/4 ounce jar black bean sauce

5 1/2 ounces Chinese
cabbage, shredded

1 Using a sharp knife, trim away any fat from the steak. Cut the steak into thin slices.

2 Heat the sunflower oil in a large preheated wok.

3 Add the steak to the wok and stir-fry for 2 minutes.

4 Using a sharp knife, peel and slice the onion.

5 Add the onion, garlic, and peas to the wok and stir-fry for a further 5 minutes.

6 Add the black bean sauce and Chinese cabbage to the mixture in the wok and heat through for a further 2 minutes, or until the cabbage has wilted.

7 Transfer to warm serving bowls and serve immediately.

COOK'S TIP

Chinese cabbage is now widely available. It looks like a pale, elongated head of lettuce with light green, tightly packed crinkly leaves.

COOK'S TIP

Buy a chunky black bean sauce if you can for the best texture and flavor.

Stir-Fried Garlic Beef with Sesame Seeds & Soy Sauce

Soy sauce and sesame seeds are classic ingredients in Chinese cookery.
Use a dark soy sauce for fuller flavor and richness.

Serves 4

INGREDIENTS

2 tbsp sesame seeds	1 green bell pepper, seeded and thinly sliced	2 tbsp dry sherry
1 pound beef fillet		4 tbsp soy sauce
2 tbsp vegetable oil	4 cloves garlic, crushed	6 scallions, sliced
		noodles, to serve

1 Heat a large wok until it is very hot.

2 Add the sesame seeds and dry-fry, stirring, for about 1–2 minutes, or until they just begin to brown. Remove from the wok and set aside until required.

3 Using a sharp knife, thinly slice the beef.

4 Heat the vegetable oil in the wok. Add the beef slices and stir-fry for 2–3 minutes, or until sealed on all sides.

5 Add the sliced bell pepper and crushed garlic to the wok and continue stir-frying for 2 minutes.

6 Add the sherry and soy sauce to the wok, together with the scallions, and allow to bubble, stirring occasionally, for about 1 minute.

7 Transfer the garlic beef stir-fry to warm serving bowls and scatter with the dry-fried sesame seeds. Serve hot with boiled noodles.

COOK'S TIP

You can spread the sesame seeds out on a cookie sheet and toast them under a preheated broiler until browned all over and giving off their aroma, if desired.

Pork Tenderloin Stir-Fry with Crunchy Satay Sauce

Satay sauce is easy to make and is one of the best known and loved sauces in Southeast Asian cooking. It is perfect with beef, chicken, or pork, as in this recipe.

Serves 4

INGREDIENTS

2–3 medium carrots
2 tbsp sunflower oil
12 ounces pork tenderloin,
  thinly sliced
1 onion, sliced
2 cloves garlic, crushed

1 yellow bell pepper, seeded
  and sliced
2^1/3 cups snow peas
1^1/2 cups fine asparagus
chopped salted peanuts, to serve

SATAY SAUCE:
6 tbsp crunchy peanut butter
6 tbsp coconut milk
1 tsp chili flakes
1 clove garlic, crushed
1 tsp tomato paste

1 Using a sharp knife, slice the carrots into thin sticks.

2 Heat the oil in a large, preheated wok. Add the pork, onion, and garlic and stir-fry for 5 minutes, or until the lamb is cooked through.

3 Add the carrots, bell pepper, snow peas, and asparagus to the wok and stir-fry for 5 minutes.

4 To make the satay sauce, place the peanut butter, coconut milk, chili flakes, garlic, and tomato paste in a small pan and heat gently, stirring, until well combined.

5 Transfer the stir-fry to warm serving plates. Spoon the satay sauce over the stir-fry and scatter with coarsely chopped peanuts. Serve immediately.

COOK'S TIP

Cook the sauce just before serving as it tends to thicken very quickly and will not be spoonable if you cook it too far in advance.

Chinese Five-spice Crispy Pork with Egg Fried Rice

Pork is coated in a spicy mixture before being fried until crisp in this recipe, and then stirred into a delicious egg rice for a very filling meal.

Serves 4

INGREDIENTS

1$\frac{1}{4}$ cups long grain white rice
2$\frac{1}{2}$ cups cold water
12 ounces pork tenderloin
2 tsp Chinese five-spice powder
4 tbsp cornstarch
3 large eggs, beaten

2 tbsp sugar
2 tbsp sunflower oil
1 onion
2 cloves garlic, crushed
1–2 medium carrots, diced
1 red bell pepper, seeded and diced

$\frac{3}{4}$ cup peas
2 tbsp butter
salt and pepper

1 Rinse the rice under cold running water. Place the rice in a large saucepan, add the cold water and a pinch of salt. Bring to a boil, cover, then reduce the heat, and simmer for about 10–15 minutes, or until all of the liquid has been absorbed and the rice is tender.

2 Meanwhile, slice the pork tenderloin into very thin pieces, using a sharp knife. Set aside until required.

3 Beat together the five-spice powder, cornstarch, 1 egg, and the sugar. Toss the pork in the mixture until coated.

4 Heat the oil in a large preheated wok. Add the pork and cook over a high heat until the pork is cooked through and crispy. Remove the pork from the wok with a slotted spoon and set aside.

5 Using a sharp knife, cut the onion into dice.

6 Add the onion, garlic, carrots, bell pepper, and peas to the wok and stir-fry for 5 minutes.

7 Return the pork to the wok, together with the cooked rice, and stir-fry for 5 minutes.

8 Heat the butter in a skillet. Add the remaining beaten eggs and cook until set. Turn out onto a clean board and slice thinly. Toss the strips of egg into the rice mixture and serve.

Spicy Pork Balls

*These small meatballs are packed with flavor and cooked
in a crunchy tomato sauce for a very quick dish.*

Serves 4

INGREDIENTS

1 pound ground pork
2 shallots, finely chopped
2 cloves garlic, crushed
1 tsp cumin seeds
$^{1}/_{2}$ tsp chili powder

$^{1}/_{2}$ cup whole-wheat bread crumbs
1 egg, beaten
2 tbsp sunflower oil
14 ounce can chopped tomatoes,
   flavored with chili

2 tbsp soy sauce
7 ounce can water chestnuts, drained
3 tbsp chopped fresh cilantro

1 Place the ground pork in a large mixing bowl. Add the shallots, garlic, cumin seeds, chili powder, bread crumbs, and beaten egg and mix together well.

2 Take small pieces of the mixture and form into balls between the palms of your hands.

3 Heat the sunflower oil in a large preheated wok. Add the pork balls to the wok and stir-fry, in batches, over a high heat for about 5 minutes, or until sealed on all sides.

4 Add the tomatoes, soy sauce, and water chestnuts and bring to a boil. Return the pork balls to the wok, reduce the heat and simmer for 15 minutes.

5 Scatter with chopped fresh cilantro, transfer to a serving dish and serve hot.

COOK'S TIP

*Add a few teaspoons of chili sauce
to a tin of chopped tomatoes, if you
can't find the flavored variety.*

COOK'S TIP

*Cilantro is also known as
Chinese parsley, but has a
much stronger flavor and should be
used with care. Parsley is not a
viable alternative; use basil if
cilantro is not available.*

Sweet & Sour Pork

Everyone loves sweet and sour pork, a classic Chinese dish. Tender pork pieces are fried and served in a crunchy sauce. This dish is perfect served with plain rice.

Serves 4

INGREDIENTS

1 pound pork tenderloin

2 tbsp sunflower oil

8 ounces zucchini

1 red onion, cut into thin wedges

2 cloves garlic, crushed

3–4 medium carrots, cut into thin sticks

1 red bell pepper, seeded and sliced

1 cup baby corn cobs

$1^{1}/_{2}$ cups button mushrooms, halved

$1^{1}/_{4}$ cups fresh pineapple, cubed

$^{1}/_{2}$ cup bean sprouts

$^{2}/_{3}$ cup pineapple juice

1 tbsp cornstarch

2 tbsp soy sauce

3 tbsp tomato ketchup

1 tbsp white wine vinegar

1 tbsp clear honey

1 Using a sharp knife, thinly slice the pork tenderloin.

2 Heat the oil in a large preheated wok.

3 Add the pork to the wok and stir-fry for 10 minutes, or until the pork is completely cooked through and beginning to turn crispy at the edges.

4 Meanwhile, cut the zucchini into thin sticks.

5 Add the onion, garlic, carrots, zucchini, bell pepper, baby corn cobs, and mushrooms to the wok and stir-fry for a further 5 minutes.

6 Add the pineapple cubes and bean sprouts to the wok and stir-fry for 2 minutes.

7 Mix together the pineapple juice, cornstarch, soy sauce, ketchup, wine vinegar and honey to make a smooth paste.

8 Pour the sweet and sour mixture into the wok and cook over a high heat, tossing frequently, until the juices thicken. Transfer the sweet and sour pork to serving bowls and serve hot.

COOK'S TIP

If you prefer a crisper coating, toss the pork in a mixture of cornstarch and egg white and deep fry in the wok in step 3.

Twice-cooked Pork with Bell Peppers

This is a really simple yet colorful dish, the trio of bell peppers offsetting the pork and sauce wonderfully.

Serves 4

INGREDIENTS

$^1/_2$ ounce Chinese dried mushrooms
1 pound pork leg steaks
2 tbsp vegetable oil
1 onion, sliced

1 red bell pepper, seeded and diced
1 green bell pepper, seeded and diced

1 yellow bell pepper, seeded and diced
4 tbsp oyster sauce

1 Place the mushrooms in a large bowl. Pour over enough boiling water to cover and let stand for 20 minutes.

2 Using a sharp knife, trim any excess fat from the pork steaks. Cut the pork into thin strips.

3 Bring a large saucepan of water to a boil. Add the pork to the boiling water and cook for 5 minutes.

4 Remove the pork from the pan with a slotted spoon and drain thoroughly.

5 Heat the oil in a large preheated wok. Add the pork to the wok and stir-fry for about 5 minutes.

6 Remove the mushrooms from the water and drain thoroughly. Discard the stalks and roughly chop the mushroom caps.

7 Add the mushrooms, onion, and the bell peppers to the wok and stir-fry for 5 minutes.

8 Stir in the oyster sauce and cook for 2-3 minutes. Transfer to serving bowls and serve immediately.

VARIATION

Use open-cap mushrooms, sliced, instead of Chinese mushrooms, if desired.

Pork with White Radish

Pork and white radish is a perfect combination, especially with the added heat of the sweet chili sauce.

Serves 4

INGREDIENTS

4 tbsp vegetable oil
1 pound pork tenderloin
1 eggplant

8 ounces white radish
2 cloves garlic, crushed

3 tbsp soy sauce
2 tbsp sweet chili sauce

---

1 Heat 2 tablespoons of the vegetable oil in a large preheated wok

2 Using a sharp knife, thinly slice the pork.

3 Add the slices of pork to the wok and stir-fry for about 5 minutes.

4 Using a sharp knife, trim and finely dice the eggplant. Peel and thinly slice the white radish.

5 Add the remaining vegetable oil to the wok.

6 Add the diced eggplant to the wok, together with the garlic and stir-fry for 5 minutes.

7 Add the white radish to the wok and stir-fry for about 2 minutes.

8 Stir the soy sauce and sweet chili sauce into the mixture in the wok and continue cooking until heated through.

9 Transfer the pork and white radish mixture to warm serving bowls or a large warm serving dish and serve immediately.

COOK'S TIP

White radish, also known as mooli or daikon, is a long white vegetable common in Chinese cooking. It is generally available in most large supermarkets. White radish is usually grated and has a milder flavor than red radish.

Meat & Poultry

Lamb with Satay Sauce

This recipe demonstrates the classic serving of lamb satay, threaded onto wooden skewers having been marinated in a delicious chili and coconut mixture.

Serves 4

INGREDIENTS

1 pound lamb loin fillet
1 tbsp mild curry paste
2/3 cup coconut milk
2 cloves garlic, crushed

1/2 tsp chili powder
1/2 tsp cumin
1 tbsp corn oil
1 onion, diced

6 tbsp crunchy peanut butter
1 tsp tomato paste
1 tsp fresh lime juice
1 1/3 cup cold water

1 Using a sharp knife, thinly slice the lamb. Place the lamb in a large dish.

2 Mix together the curry paste, coconut milk, garlic, chili powder, and cumin in a bowl.

3 Pour the mixture over the lamb, toss well, cover, and marinate for 30 minutes.

4 Meanwhile, make the satay sauce. Heat the oil in a large wok. Add the onion and stir-fry for 5 minutes, then reduce the heat, and cook for 5 minutes.

5 Add the peanut butter, tomato paste, lime juice, and cold water to the wok, stirring well to combine.

6 Thread the lamb onto wooden skewers, reserving the marinade.

7 Broil the lamb skewers under a preheated broiler for 6–8 minutes, turning once.

8 Add the reserved marinade to the wok, bring to a boil, and cook for 5 minutes. Serve the lamb skewers with the satay sauce.

COOK'S TIP

Soak the wooden skewers in cold water for 30 minutes before broiling to prevent the skewers from burning.

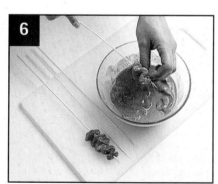

Stir-Fried Lamb with Black Bean Sauce & Mixed Bell Peppers

Red onions add great color to recipes and are perfect in this dish, combining with the colors of the bell peppers.

Serves 4

INGREDIENTS

1 pound lamb neck fillet or boneless
   leg of lamb chops
1 egg white, lightly beaten
4 tbsp cornstarch
1 tsp Chinese five-spice powder
3 tbsp sunflower oil

1 red onion
1 red bell pepper, seeded
   and sliced
1 green bell pepper, seeded
   and sliced

1 yellow or orange bell pepper,
   seeded and sliced
5 tbsp black bean sauce
boiled rice or noodles, to serve

1 Using a sharp knife, slice the lamb into very thin strips.

2 Mix the egg white, cornstarch, and Chinese five-spice powder together in a large bowl. Toss the lamb strips in the mixture until evenly coated.

3 Heat the oil in a large preheated wok. Add the lamb and stir-fry over a high heat for 5 minutes, or until it begins to crispen around the edges.

4 Using a sharp knife, slice the red onion. Add the onion and bell pepper slices to the wok and stir-fry for 5–6 minutes, or until the vegetables just begin to soften.

5 Stir the black bean sauce into the mixture in the wok and heat through.

6 Transfer the lamb and sauce to warm serving plates and serve hot with freshly boiled rice or noodles.

COOK'S TIP

Take care when frying the lamb as the cornstarch mixture may cause it to stick to the wok. Move the lamb around the wok constantly during stir-frying.

Scallion & Lamb Stir-Fry with Oyster Sauce

This really is a speedy dish, lamb leg steaks being perfect for the short cooking time.

Serves 4

INGREDIENTS

1 pound lamb leg steaks
1 tsp ground Szechuan peppercorns
1 tbsp peanut oil

2 cloves garlic, crushed
8 scallions, sliced
2 tbsp dark soy sauce

6 tbsp oyster sauce
6 ounces Chinese cabbage
shrimp crackers, to serve

1 Using a sharp knife, remove any excess fat from the lamb. Slice the lamb thinly.

2 Sprinkle the ground Szechuan peppercorns over the meat and toss together until well combined.

3 Heat the oil in a preheated wok. Add the lamb and stir-fry for 5 minutes.

4 Mix the garlic, scallions, and soy sauce, add to the wok, and stir-fry for 2 minutes.

5 Add the oyster sauce and Chinese cabbage and stir-fry for a further 2 minutes, or until the leaves have wilted and the juices are bubbling.

6 Transfer the stir-fry to warm serving bowls and serve hot.

COOK'S TIP

Shrimp crackers consist of compressed slivers of shrimp and flour paste. They expand when deep-fried.

COOK'S TIP

Oyster sauce is made from oysters which are cooked in brine and soy sauce. Sold in bottles, it will keep in the refrigerator for months.

Curried Stir-Fried Lamb with Diced Potatoes

This dish is very filling, only requiring a simple vegetable accompaniment or bread.

Serves 4

INGREDIENTS

1 pound potatoes, diced
1 pound lean lamb, cubed
2 tbsp medium hot curry paste
3 tbsp sunflower oil

1 onion, sliced
1 eggplant, diced
2 cloves garlic, crushed
1 tbsp grated fresh ginger root

$^2/_3$ cup lamb or beef stock
2 tbsp chopped fresh cilantro

1 Bring a large saucepan of lightly salted water to a boil. Add the potatoes and cook over a medium heat for 10 minutes. Remove the potatoes from the saucepan with a slotted spoon and drain thoroughly.

2 Meanwhile, place the lamb in a large mixing bowl. Add the curry paste and mix until thoroughly combined.

3 Heat the sunflower oil in a large preheated wok.

4 Lower the heat slightly, add the onion, eggplant, garlic, and ginger to the wok, and stir-fry for about 5 minutes.

5 Add the lamb to the wok and stir-fry for a further 5 minutes.

6 Add the lamb or beef stock and drained cooked potatoes to the wok, bring to a boil, and simmer for 30 minutes, or until the lamb is tender and completely cooked through.

7 Transfer the stir-fry to warm serving dishes and scatter with chopped fresh cilantro. Serve immediately.

COOK'S TIP

The wok is an ancient Chinese invention, the name coming from the Cantonese, meaning a "cooking vessel."

Garlic-infused Lamb with Soy Sauce

*The long marinating time allows the garlic to really penetrate the meat,
creating a much more flavorful dish.*

Serves 4

INGREDIENTS

1 pound lamb loin fillet
2 cloves garlic
2 tbsp peanut oil

3 tbsp dry sherry or Chinese rice wine
3 tbsp dark soy
1 tsp cornstarch

2 tbsp cold water
2 tbsp butter

1 Using a sharp knife, make small slits in the flesh of the lamb.

2 Carefully peel the cloves of garlic and cut them into slices, using a sharp knife.

3 Push the slices of garlic into the slits in the lamb. Place the garlic-infused lamb in a shallow dish.

4 Drizzle 1 tablespoon each of the oil, sherry, and soy sauce over the lamb, cover and set aside to marinate for at least 1 hour, preferably overnight.

5 Using a sharp knife, thinly slice the marinated lamb.

6 Heat the remaining oil in a preheated wok. Add the lamb and stir-fry for 5 minutes.

7 Add the marinade juices and the remaining sherry and soy sauce to the wok and allow the juices to bubble for 5 minutes.

8 Mix the cornstarch with the cold water to make a smooth paste. Add the cornstarch mixture to the wok and cook, stirring occasionally, until the juices start to thicken.

9 Cut the butter into small pieces. Add the butter to the wok and stir until the butter melts. Transfer to serving dishes and serve immediately.

COOK'S TIP

Adding the butter at the end of the recipe gives a glossy, rich sauce which is ideal with the lamb.

Thai-Style Lamb with Lime Leaves

*Peanut oil is used here for flavor—it is
a common oil used for stir-frying.*

Serves 4

INGREDIENTS

2 red Thai chilies
2 tbsp peanut oil
2 cloves garlic, crushed
4 shallots, chopped
2 stalks lemon grass, sliced

6 lime leaves
1 tbsp tamarind paste
2 tbsp palm sugar or brown sugar
1 pound lean lamb (leg or loin fillet)
2$\frac{1}{2}$ cups coconut milk

6 ounces cherry tomatoes, halved
1 tbsp chopped fresh cilantro
fragrant rice, to serve

1 Using a sharp knife, seed and very finely chop the Thai red chilies.

2 Heat the peanut oil in a large preheated wok.

3 Add the garlic, shallots, lemon grass, lime leaves, tamarind paste, palm sugar or brown sugar, and chilies to the wok and stir-fry for about 2 minutes.

4 Using a sharp knife, cut the lamb into thin strips or cubes.

5 Add the lamb to the wok and stir-fry for about 5 minutes, tossing well so that the lamb is evenly coated in the spice mixture.

6 Pour the coconut milk into the wok and bring to a boil. Reduce the heat and simmer for 20 minutes.

7 Add the cherry tomatoes and chopped fresh cilantro to the wok and simmer for 5 minutes. Transfer to individual warm serving plates and serve hot with fragrant rice.

COOK'S TIP

Thai limes, also known as makut, *differ from the common lime in that the leaves are highly scented and the fruits resemble knobby balls. Thai lime leaves are often used in cooking for flavor.*

Stir-Fried Lamb with Orange

Oranges and lamb are a great combination because the citrus flavor offsets the fattier, fuller flavor of the lamb.

Serves 4

INGREDIENTS

1 pound ground lamb
2 cloves garlic, crushed
1 tsp cumin seeds
1 tsp ground coriander

1 red onion, sliced
finely grated zest and juice of
    1 orange
2 tbsp soy sauce

1 orange, peeled and segmented
salt and pepper
snipped fresh chives, to garnish

1 Add the ground lamb to a preheated wok. Dry fry the ground lamb for 5 minutes, or until the meat is evenly browned. Drain away any excess fat from the wok.

2 Add the garlic, cumin seeds, coriander, and red onion to the wok and stir-fry for a further 5 minutes.

3 Stir in the finely grated orange zest and juice and the soy sauce, cover, reduce the heat, and simmer, stirring occasionally, for 15 minutes.

4 Remove the lid, raise the heat, add the orange segments, and salt and pepper to taste and heat through for a further 2–3 minutes.

5 Transfer to warm serving plates and garnish with snipped fresh chives. Serve immediately.

COOK'S TIP

If you wish to serve wine with your meal, try light, dry white wines and lighter Burgundy-style red wines as they blend well with Asian food.

VARIATION

Use lime or lemon juice and zest instead of the orange, if wished.

Lamb's Liver with Green Bell Peppers & Sherry

This is a richly flavored dish which is great served with plain rice or noodles to soak up the delicious juices.

Serves 4

INGREDIENTS

1 pound lamb's liver
2 tbsp cornstarch
2 tbsp peanut oil
1 onion, sliced

2 cloves garlic, crushed
2 green bell peppers, seeded and sliced
2 tbsp tomato paste

3 tbsp dry sherry
1 tbsp cornstarch
2 tbsp soy sauce

1 Using a sharp knife, trim any excess fat and the membranes from the lamb's liver. Slice the lamb's liver into thin, even-size strips.

2 Place the cornstarch in a large bowl.

3 Add the strips of lamb's liver to the cornstarch and toss well until coated evenly all over.

4 Heat the peanut oil in a large preheated wok.

5 Add the lamb's liver, onion, garlic, and green bell pepper to the wok and stir-fry for 6–7 minutes, or until the lamb's liver is just cooked through and the vegetables are tender.

6 Mix together the tomato paste, sherry, cornstarch, and soy sauce to male a smooth paste. Stir the mixture into the wok and cook for a further 2 minutes, or until the juices have thickened. Transfer to warm serving bowls and serve immediately.

VARIATION

Use rice wine instead of the sherry for a really authentic Asian flavor. Chinese rice wine is made from glutinous rice and is also known as "yellow wine" because of its golden color. The best variety, from Southeast China, is called Shao Hsing *or* Shaoxing.

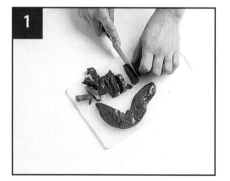

Fish & Seafood

Throughout the Far Eastern countries,
fish and seafood play a major role in the diet, as they
are both plentiful and healthy. There are many
different ways of cooking fish and seafood in a
wok—they may be steamed, deep-fried, or stir-fried
with a range of delicious spices and sauces.

Japan is famed for its sushimi or raw fish, but this is
just one of the wide range of fish dishes served. Fish
and seafood are offered at every meal in Japan, many of
them cooked in a wok. Many unusual and tasty dishes
are offered in this chapter, combining fish and seafood
with aromatic herbs and spices, pastes and sauces.

When buying fish and seafood for the recipes in this
chapter, freshness is imperative to flavor, so be
sure to buy and use it as soon as possible,
preferably the same day.

Teriyaki Stir-Fried Salmon with Crispy Leeks

Teriyaki is a wonderful Japanese dish which is delicous when made with salmon and served on a bed of crispy leeks.

Serves 4

INGREDIENTS

1 pound salmon fillet, skinned
2 tbsp sweet soy sauce
2 tbsp tomato ketchup

1 tsp rice wine vinegar
1 tbsp sugar
1 clove garlic, crushed

4 tbsp corn oil
1 leek, thinly shredded
finely chopped red chilies, to garnish

1 Using a sharp knife, cut the salmon into slices. Place the slices of salmon in a shallow nonmetallic dish.

2 Mix together the soy sauce, tomato ketchup, rice wine vinegar, sugar, and garlic.

3 Pour the mixture over the salmon, toss well, and marinate for about 30 minutes.

4 Meanwhile, heat 3 tablespoons of the corn oil in a large preheated wok.

5 Add the leeks to the wok and stir-fry over a medium high heat for about 10 minutes, or until the leeks become crispy and tender.

6 Using a slotted spoon, carefully remove the leeks from the wok and transfer to warm serving plates.

7 Add the remaining oil to the wok. Add the salmon and the marinade to the wok and cook for 2 minutes. Spoon it over the leeks, garnish, and serve immediately.

VARIATION

You can use a fillet of beef instead of the salmon, if wished.

Stir-Fried Salmon with Pineapple

Presentation plays a major part in Chinese cooking and this dish demonstrates this perfectly with the wonderful combination of colors.

Serves 4

INGREDIENTS

1 cup baby corn cobs, halved

2 tbsp sunflower oil

1 red onion, sliced

1 orange bell pepper, seeded and sliced

1 green bell pepper, seeded and sliced

1 pound salmon fillet, skin removed

1 tbsp paprika

8 ounce can cubed pineapple, drained

1/2 cup bean sprouts

2 tbsp tomato ketchup

2 tbsp soy sauce

2 tbsp medium sherry

1 tsp cornstarch

1 Using a sharp knife, cut the baby corn cobs in half.

2 Heat the sunflower oil in a large preheated wok. Add the onion, bell peppers, and baby corn cobs to the wok and stir-fry for 5 minutes.

3 Rinse the salmon fillet under cold running water and pat dry with absorbent paper towels.

4 Cut the salmon flesh into thin strips and place in a large bowl. Sprinkle with the paprika and toss until well coated.

5 Add the salmon to the wok, together with the pineapple, and stir-fry for a further 2–3 minutes or until the fish is tender.

6 Add the bean sprouts to the wok and toss well.

7 Mix together the tomato ketchup, soy sauce, sherry, and cornstarch. Add the mixture to the wok and cook until the juices thicken. Transfer to warm serving plates and serve immediately.

VARIATION

You can use trout fillets instead of the salmon as an alternative, if wished.

Tuna & Vegetable Stir-Fry

Fresh tuna is a dark, meaty fish and is now widely available at fresh fish counters.
It lends itself perfectly to the rich flavors in this recipe.

Serves 4

INGREDIENTS

3–4 medium carrots
2 tbsp corn oil
1 onion, sliced
2¹/₂ cups snow peas
1³/₄ cups baby corn cobs, halved

1 pound fresh tuna
2 tbsp fish sauce
1 tbsp palm sugar or brown sugar
finely grated zest and juice of
  1 orange

2 tbsp sherry
1 tsp cornstarch
rice or noodles, to serve

1 Using a sharp knife, cut the carrots into thin sticks.

2 Heat the corn oil in a large preheated wok.

3 Add the onion, carrots, snow peas, and baby corn cobs to the wok and stir-fry for 5 minutes.

4 Using a sharp knife, thinly slice the tuna.

5 Add the tuna to the wok and stir-fry for 2–3 minutes, or until the tuna turns opaque.

6 Mix together the fish sauce, palm sugar or brown sugar, orange zest and juice, sherry, and cornstarch.

7 Pour the mixture over the tuna and vegetables and cook for 2 minutes, or until the juices thicken. Serve with rice or noodles.

COOK'S TIP

Baby corn cobs have a deliciously sweet fragrance and flavor. They are available both fresh and canned.

VARIATION

Try using swordfish steaks instead of the tuna. Swordfish steaks are now widely available and are similar in texture to tuna.

Stir-Fried Cod with Mango

Fish and fruit is a classic combination, and in this recipe a tropical flavor is added which gives a great scented taste to the dish.

Serves 4

INGREDIENTS

2–3 medium carrots	1 pound skinless cod fillet	1 tbsp lime juice
2 tbsp vegetable oil	1 ripe mango	1 tbsp chopped cilantro
1 onion, sliced	1 tsp cornstarch	
1 red bell pepper, seeded and sliced	1 tbsp soy sauce	
1 green bell pepper, seeded and sliced	1⅓ cup tropical fruit juice	

1 Using a sharp knife, slice the carrots into thin sticks.

2 Heat the vegetable oil in a preheated wok.

3 Add the onions, carrots, and bell peppers to the wok and stir-fry for 5 minutes.

4 Using a sharp knife, cut the cod into small cubes.

5 Peel the mango, then carefully remove the flesh from the central pit. Cut the flesh into thin slices.

6 Add the cod and mango to the wok and stir-fry for a further 4–5 minutes, or until the fish is cooked through. Do not stir the mixture too much or you may break the fish up.

7 Mix the cornstarch, soy sauce, fruit juice, and lime juice in a small bowl.

8 Pour the cornstarch mixture over the stir-fry and allow the mixture to bubble and the juices to thicken. Scatter with cilantro, transfer to a warm serving dish, and serve immediately.

VARIATION

You can use papaya as an alternative to the mango, if wished.

Stir-Fried Gingered Monkfish

This dish is a real treat and is perfect for special occasions. Monkfish has a tender flavor which is ideal with asparagus, chili, and ginger.

Serves 4

INGREDIENTS

1 pound monkfish
1 tbsp freshly grated ginger root
2 tbsp sweet chili sauce

1 tbsp corn oil
1 cup fine asparagus
3 scallions, sliced

1 tsp sesame oil

1 Remove the membrane from the monkfish, then using a sharp knife, slice the flesh into thin flat rounds.

2 Mix the ginger with the chili sauce in a small bowl.

3 Brush the ginger and chili sauce mixture over the monkfish pieces.

4 Heat the corn oil in a large preheated wok.

5 Add the monkfish, asparagus, and scallions to the wok and stir-fry for about 5 minutes.

6 Remove the wok from the heat, drizzle the sesame oil over the stir-fry, and toss well to combine.

7 Transfer to warm serving plates and serve immediately.

COOK'S TIP

Some recipes specify to grate ginger before it is cooked with other ingredients. To do this, just peel the flesh and rub it at a 45 degree angle up and down on the fine section of a metal grater, or use a special wooden or ceramic ginger grater.

VARIATION

Monkfish is quite expensive, but it is well worth using it as it has a wonderful flavor and texture. Otherwise, could use cubes of chunky cod fillet instead.

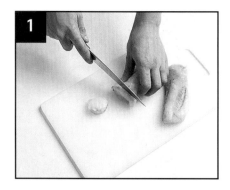

Braised Fish Fillets

Any white fish, such as lemon sole or flounder, is ideal for this delicious dish. Cornstarch paste is made by mixing 1 part cornstarch with about 1½ parts cold water.

Serves 4

INGREDIENTS

3–4 small Chinese dried mushrooms
10½–12 ounces fish fillets
1 tsp salt
½ egg white, lightly beaten
1 tsp cornstarch paste
2½ cups vegetable oil
1 tsp finely chopped ginger root

2 scallions, finely chopped
1 garlic clove, finely chopped
½ small green bell pepper, seeded
  and cut into small cubes
½ small carrot, thinly sliced
½ cup canned sliced bamboo shoots,
  rinsed and drained

½ tsp sugar
1 tbsp light soy sauce
1 tsp rice wine or dry sherry
1 tbsp chili bean sauce
2–3 tbsp Chinese stock or water
a few drops of sesame oil

1 Soak the dried mushrooms in a bowl of warm water for 30 minutes. Drain the mushrooms thoroughly on paper towels, reserving the soaking water for stock or soup. Squeeze the mushrooms to extract all of the moisture, cut off and discard any hard stems, and slice the caps thinly.

2 Cut the fish into bite-size pieces, then place in a shallow dish, and mix with a pinch of salt, the egg white, and cornstarch paste, turning the fish to coat well.

3 Heat the oil in a preheated wok. Add the fish pieces to the wok and deep-fry for about 1 minute. Remove the fish pieces with a slotted spoon and drain on paper towels.

4 Pour off the excess oil, leaving about 1 tablespoon in the wok. Add the ginger, scallions, and garlic to flavor the oil for a few seconds, then add the bell pepper, carrots, and bamboo shoots and stir-fry for about 1 minute.

5 Add the sugar, soy sauce, wine, chili bean sauce, stock or water, and the remaining salt and bring to a boil. Add the fish pieces, stir to coat well with the sauce, and braise for 1 minute.

6 Sprinkle with sesame oil, transfer to a warm serving dish, and serve immediately.

Fried Fish with Coconut & Basil

Fish curries are sensational and this Thai curry is no exception. Red curry and coconut are fantastic flavors with the fried fish.

Serves 4

INGREDIENTS

2 tbsp vegetable oil
1 pound skinless cod fillet
¼ cup seasoned all-purpose flour
1 clove garlic, crushed

2 tbsp red Thai curry paste
1 tbsp fish sauce
1¼ cups coconut milk
6 ounces cherry tomatoes, halved

20 fresh basil leaves
fragrant rice, to serve

1 Heat the vegetable oil in a large preheated wok.

2 Using a sharp knife, cut the fish into large cubes, taking care to remove any bones with a pair of tweezers.

3 Place the seasoned flour in a bowl. Add the cubes of fish and mix until well coated.

4 Add the coated fish to the wok and stir-fry over a high heat for 3–4 minutes, or until the fish just begins to brown at the edges.

5 Mix together the garlic, curry paste, fish sauce, and coconut milk in a bowl. Pour the mixture over the fish and bring to a boil.

6 Add the tomatoes to the mixture in the wok and simmer for 5 minutes.

7 Roughly chop or tear the fresh basil leaves. Add the basil to the wok, stir carefully to combine, taking care not to break up the cubes of fish.

8 Transfer to serving plates and serve hot with fragrant rice.

COOK'S TIP

Take care not to overcook the dish once the tomatoes are added, otherwise they will break down and the skins will come away.

Coconut Shrimp

These crispy, fried shrimp look fantastic and taste just as good. Fan-tail shrimp make any meal a special occasion, especially when cooked in such a delicious crispy coating.

Serves 4

INGREDIENTS

¹/₂ cup shredded coconut	finely grated zest of 1 lime	lemon wedges, to garnish
¹/₂ cup fresh white bread crumbs	1 egg white	
1 tsp Chinese five-spice powder	1 pound fan-tail shrimp	
¹/₂ tsp salt	sunflower or corn oil, for frying	

1 Put the shredded coconut, white bread crumbs, Chinese five-spice powder, salt, and finely grated lime zest into a medium-size bowl and thoroughly mix together.

2 Lightly beat the egg white in a separate bowl.

3 Rinse the shrimp under cold running water and pat dry with absorbent paper towels.

4 Dip the shrimp into the egg white, then into the coconut crumb mixture, so that they are evenly coated.

5 Heat about 2 inches of sunflower or corn oil in a large preheated wok.

6 Add the shrimp to the wok and stir-fry for about 5 minutes or until golden colored and crispy.

7 Remove the shrimp with a slotted spoon, transfer to absorbent paper towels, and let drain thoroughly.

8 Transfer the coconut shrimp to warm serving dishes and garnish with lemon wedges. Serve immediately.

COOK'S TIP

Serve the shrimp with a soy sauce or chili sauce, if you wish.

Shrimp Omelet

*This really is a meal in minutes, combining many
Chinese ingredients for a truly tasty dish.*

Serves 4

INGREDIENTS

2 tbsp sunflower oil	$^1/_2$ cup bean sprouts	6 eggs
4 scallions, sliced	1 tsp cornstarch	
12 ounces peeled shrimp	1 tbsp light soy sauce	

1 Heat the sunflower oil in a large preheated wok.

2 Using a sharp knife, trim the scallions and cut them into thin slices.

3 Add the shrimp, scallions, and bean sprouts to the wok and stir-fry for 2 minutes.

4 Mix together the cornstarch and soy sauce in a small bowl.

5 Beat together the eggs and 3 tablespoons of cold water and then blend with the cornstarch and soy mixture.

6 Add the egg mixture to the wok and cook for about 5–6 minutes, or until the mixture is just setting.

7 Transfer the omelet to a serving plate and cut into quarters to serve.

COOK'S TIP

*It is important to use fresh bean
sprouts for this dish as the canned
ones don't have the crunchy
texture necessary.*

VARIATION

*Add any other vegetables of your
choice, such as grated carrot or
cooked peas, to the omelet in step 3,
if you wish.*

Shrimp with Spicy Tomatoes

Basil and tomatoes are ideal flavorings for shrimp
spiced with cumin seeds and garlic.

Serves 4

INGREDIENTS

2 tbsp corn oil
1 onion
2 cloves garlic, crushed
1 tsp cumin seeds

1 tbsp sugar
14 ounce can chopped tomatoes
1 tbsp sun-dried tomato paste
1 tbsp chopped fresh basil

1 pound peeled jumbo shrimp
salt and pepper

1 Heat the corn oil in a large preheated wok.

2 Using a sharp knife, finely chop the onion.

3 Add the onion and garlic to the wok and stir-fry for 2–3 minutes, or until softened.

4 Stir in the cumin seeds and stir-fry for 1 minute.

5 Add the sugar, chopped tomatoes, and sun-dried tomato paste to the wok. Bring the mixture to a boil, then reduce the heat and simmer the sauce for about 10 minutes.

6 Add the basil, shrimp, and salt and pepper to taste to the mixture in the wok. Increase the heat and cook for a further 2–3 minutes or until the shrimp are completely cooked through.

COOK'S TIP

Sun-dried tomato paste has a much more intense flavor than that of normal tomato paste. It adds a distinctive intensity to any tomato-based dish.

COOK'S TIP

Always heat your wok before you add oil or other ingredients. This will prevent anything from sticking to it.

Shrimp with Crispy Ginger

Crispy ginger is a wonderful garnish which offsets the spicy shrimp both visually and in flavor.

Serves 4

INGREDIENTS

2 -inch piece fresh ginger root
oil, for frying
1 onion, diced
3–4 medium carrots, diced

$^1/_2$ cup frozen peas
$^1/_2$ cup bean sprouts
1 pound peeled jumbo shrimp
1 tsp Chinese five-spice powder

1 tbsp tomato paste
1 tbsp soy sauce

1 Using a sharp knife, peel the ginger and slice it into very thin sticks.

2 Heat about 1 inch of oil in a large preheated wok.

3 Add the ginger to the wok and stir-fry for 1 minute, or until the ginger is crispy. Remove the ginger with a slotted spoon and let drain on absorbent paper towels. Set aside.

4 Drain all of the oil from the wok except for about 2 tablespoons.

5 Add the onions and carrots to the wok and stir-fry for 5 minutes.

6 Add the peas and bean sprouts to the wok and stir-fry for 2 minutes.

7 Rinse the shrimp under cold running water and pat dry thoroughly with absorbent paper towels.

8 Mix together the five-spice powder, tomato paste, and soy sauce. Brush the mixture all over the shrimp.

9 Add the shrimp to the wok and stir-fry for a further 2 minutes, or until the shrimp are completely cooked through. Transfer the shrimp mixture to a warm serving bowl and top with the reserved crispy ginger. Serve immediately.

VARIATION

Use slices of white fish instead of the shrimp as an alternative, if you wish.

Vegetables with Shrimp & Egg

In this recipe, a light Chinese omelet is shredded and tossed back into the dish before serving.

Serves 4

INGREDIENTS

8 ounces zucchini
3 tbsp vegetable oil
2 eggs
3–4 medium carrots, grated

1 onion, sliced
$3/4$ cup bean sprouts
8 ounces peeled shrimp
2 tbsp soy sauce

pinch of Chinese five-spice powder
$1/4$ cup peanuts, chopped
2 tbsp fresh chopped cilantro

1 Trim and finely grate the zucchini.

2 Heat 1 tablespoon of the oil in a large preheated wok.

3 Lightly beat the eggs with 2 tablespoons of cold water. Pour the mixture into the wok and cook for 2–3 minutes or until the egg sets.

4 Remove the omelet from the wok and transfer to a clean board. Fold the omelet, cut it into thin strips, and set aside until it is required.

5 Add the remaining oil to the wok. Add the carrots, onion, and zucchini and stir-fry for 5 minutes.

6 Add the bean sprouts and shrimp to the wok and cook for a further 2 minutes, or until the shrimp are completely heated through.

7 Add the soy sauce, five-spice powder and peanuts to the wok, together with the strips of omelet, and heat through. Garnish with chopped fresh cilantro and serve immediately.

COOK'S TIP

The water is mixed with the egg in step 3 for a lighter, less rubbery omelet.

Stir-fried Crab Claws with Chili

Crab claws are frequently used in Chinese cooking, and look sensational.
They are perfect with this delicious chili sauce.

Serves 4

INGREDIENTS

1 pound 9 ounces crab claws
1 tbsp corn oil
2 cloves garlic, crushed
1 tbsp grated fresh ginger root

3 red chilies, seeded and
  finely chopped
2 tbsp sweet chili sauce
3 tbsp tomato ketchup

1¼ cups fish stock
1 tbsp cornstarch
salt and pepper
1 tbsp fresh chives, snipped

1 Gently crack the crab claws with a nut cracker. This process will allow the flavors of the chili, garlic, and ginger to fully penetrate the crab meat.

2 Heat the corn oil in a large preheated wok.

3 Add the crab claws to the wok and stir-fry for about 5 minutes.

4 Add the garlic, ginger, and chilies to the wok and stir-fry for 1 minute, tossing the crab claws to coat all over.

5 Mix together the chili sauce, tomato ketchup, fish stock, and cornstarch in a small bowl.

6 Add the chili and cornstarch mixture to the wok and cook, stirring occasionally, until the sauce starts to thicken. Season with salt and pepper to taste.

7 Transfer the crab claws and chili sauce to warm serving dishes and garnish with plenty of snipped fresh chives. Serve immediately.

COOK'S TIP

If crab claws are not easily available, use a whole crab, cut into eight pieces, instead.

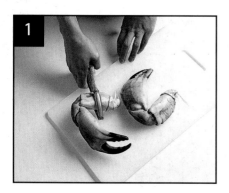

Chinese Cabbage with Shiitake Mushrooms & Crab Meat

Chinese cabbage and crab meat make a great combination, as both have a delicate flavor which is enhanced by the coconut milk in this recipe.

Serves 4

INGREDIENTS

8 ounces shiitake mushrooms
2 tbsp vegetable oil
2 cloves garlic, crushed
6 scallions, sliced

1 head Chinese cabbage, shredded
1 tbsp mild curry paste
6 tbsp coconut milk

7 ounce can white crab meat, drained
1 tsp chili flakes

1 Using a sharp knife, cut the the mushrooms into slices.

2 Heat the vegetable oil in a large preheated wok.

3 Add the mushrooms and garlic to the wok and stir-fry for 3 minutes, or until the mushrooms have softened.

4 Add the scallions and shredded Chinese cabbage to the wok and stir-fry until the leaves have wilted.

5 Mix together the mild curry paste and coconut milk in a small bowl.

6 Add the curry paste and coconut milk mixture to the wok, together with the crab meat and chili flakes. Mix together until thoroughly combined and heat through until the juices start to bubble.

7 Transfer to warm serving bowls and then serve immediately.

COOK'S TIP

Shiitake mushrooms are now readily available in the fresh vegetable section of most large supermarkets.

Stir-Fried Lettuce with Mussels & Lemon Grass

Mussels require careful preparation, but very little cooking. They are available fresh or in vacuum packs when out of season.

Serves 4

INGREDIENTS

2^1/$_4$ pounds mussels in their shells, scrubbed and debearded

2 stalks lemon grass, thinly sliced

2 tbsp lemon juice

^{1}/$_2$ cup water

2 tbsp butter

1 iceberg lettuce

finely grated zest of 1 lemon

2 tbsp oyster sauce

---

1 Discard any mussels that do not shut when sharply tapped. Place the mussels in a large saucepan.

2 Add the lemon grass, lemon juice, and water to the pan, cover, and cook for 5 minutes, or until the mussels have opened. Discard any that have not opened.

3 Carefully remove the cooked mussels from their shells.

4 Heat the butter in a large preheated wok.

5 Add the lettuce and lemon zest to the wok and stir-fry for 2 minutes, or until the lettuce begins to wilt.

6 Add the oyster sauce to the mixture in the wok, stir, and heat through. Serve immediately.

COOK'S TIP

Lemon grass with its citrus fragrance and lemon flavor looks like a fibrous scallion and is often used in Thai cooking.

COOK'S TIP

When using fresh mussels, be sure to discard any opened mussels before scrubbing and any unopened mussels after cooking.

Mussels in Black Bean Sauce with Spinach

This dish looks so impressive, the combination of colors making it look almost too good to eat!

Serves 4

INGREDIENTS

12 ounces leeks
12 ounces cooked green-lipped
  mussels, shelled
1 tsp cumin seeds

2 tbsp vegetable oil
2 cloves garlic, crushed
1 red bell pepper, seeded and sliced
$3/4$ cup canned bamboo shoots,
  drained

6 ounces baby spinach
$5^3/4$ ounce jar black bean sauce

1 Using a sharp knife, trim the leeks and shred them.

2 Place the mussels in a large bowl, sprinkle with the cumin seeds, and toss well to coat all over.

3 Heat the vegetable oil in a large preheated wok.

4 Add the leeks, garlic, and red bell pepper to the wok and stir-fry for 5 minutes, or until the vegetables are tender.

5 Add the bamboo shoots, baby spinach leaves, and cooked green-lipped mussels to the wok and stir-fry for about 2 minutes.

6 Pour the black bean sauce over the ingredients in the wok, toss well to coat all over, and simmer for a few seconds, stirring occasionally.

7 Transfer the stir-fry to warm serving bowls and serve immediately.

COOK'S TIP

If fresh green-lipped mussels are not available, they can be bought shelled in cans and jars from most large supermarkets.

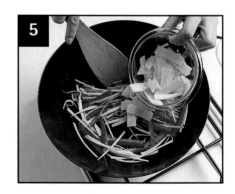

Scallop Pancakes

Scallops, like most shellfish require very little cooking, and this original and delicious dish is a perfect example of how to use shellfish to its full potential.

Serves 4

INGREDIENTS

$^3/_4$ cup fine green beans
1 red chili
1 pound scallops, without corals

1 egg
3 scallions, sliced
$^1/_2$ cup rice flour

1 tbsp fish sauce
oil, for frying
sweet chili dip, to serve

1 Using a sharp knife, trim the green beans and slice them very thinly.

2 Using a sharp knife, seed and very finely chop the red chili.

3 Bring a small saucepan of lightly salted water to a boil. Add the green beans to the pan and cook for 3–4 minutes, or until just softened.

4 Roughly chop the scallops and place them in a large bowl. Add the cooked beans to the scallops.

5 Mix the egg with the scallions, rice flour, fish sauce, and chili until thoroughly combined. Add to the scallops and mix well.

6 Heat about 1 inch of oil in a large preheated wok. Add a ladleful of the mixture to the wok and cook for 5 minutes, until golden and set. Remove the pancake from the wok and let drain on absorbent paper towels. Repeat with the remaining pancake mixture.

7 Serve the pancakes hot with a sweet chili dip.

VARIATION

You could use shrimp or shelled clams instead of the scallops, if wished.

Seared Scallops with Butter Sauce

Scallops have a terrific, subtle flavor which is complemented by this buttery sauce.

Serves 4

INGREDIENTS

1 pound scallops, without corals	2 tbsp vegetable oil	3 tbsp sweet soy sauce
6 scallions	1 green chili, seeded and sliced	2 tbsp butter, diced

1 Rinse the scallops well under cold running water, then pat the scallops dry with absorbent paper towels.

2 Using a sharp knife, slice each scallop in half horizontally.

3 Using a sharp knife, trim and thinly slice the scallions.

4 Heat the vegetable oil in a large preheated wok.

5 Add the sliced chili, scallions, and scallops to the wok and stir-fry over a high heat for about 4–5 minutes, or until the scallops are just cooked through and have become slightly opaque.

6 Add the soy sauce and butter to the scallop stir-fry and heat through until the butter melts.

7 Transfer to warm serving bowls and serve hot.

COOK'S TIP

If you buy scallops on the shell, slide a knife underneath the membrane to loosen and cut off the tough muscle that holds the scallop to the shell. Discard the black stomach sac and intestinal vein.

COOK'S TIP

Use frozen scallops if desired, but make sure they are completely thawed before cooking. In addition, do not overcook them, as they will easily disintegrate.

Stir-Fried Oysters with Bean Curd, Lemon, & Cilantro

Oysters are often eaten raw, but are delicious when quickly cooked, as in this recipe, and mixed with salt and citrus flavors.

Serves 4

INGREDIENTS

8 ounces leeks

12 ounces bean curd

2 tbsp sunflower oil

12 ounces shelled oysters

2 tbsp fresh lemon juice

1 tsp cornstarch

2 tbsp light soy sauce

1/3 cup fish stock

2 tbsp chopped fresh cilantro

1 tsp finely grated lemon zest

1 Using a sharp knife, trim and slice the leeks.

2 Cut the bean curd into bite-size pieces.

3 Heat the sunflower oil in a large preheated wok.

4 Add the leeks to the wok and stir-fry for about 2 minutes.

5 Add the bean curd and oysters to the wok and stir-fry for 1–2 minutes.

6 Mix together the lemon juice, cornstarch, light soy sauce, and fish stock to a smooth paste in a small bowl.

7 Pour the cornstarch mixture into the wok and cook, stirring occasionally, until the juices start to thicken.

8 Transfer the stir-fry to warm serving bowls and scatter the chopped cilantro and grated lemon zest on top. Serve the stir-fry immediately.

VARIATION

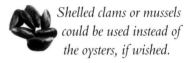

Shelled clams or mussels could be used instead of the oysters, if wished.

Crispy Fried Squid with Salt & Pepper

Squid tubes are classically used in Chinese cooking and are most attractive when presented as in the following recipe.

Serves 4

INGREDIENTS

1 pound squid, cleaned
4 tbsp cornstarch
1 tsp salt

1 tsp freshly ground black pepper
1 tsp chili flakes
peanut oil, for frying

dipping sauce, to serve

1 Using a sharp knife, remove the tentacles from the squid and trim. Slice the bodies down one side and open out to give a flat piece.

2 Score the flat pieces with a criss-cross pattern, then cut each piece into 4.

3 Mix together the cornstarch, salt, pepper, and chili flakes.

4 Place the salt and pepper mixture in a large plastic bag. Add the squid pieces, tie the top tightly, and shake the bag thoroughly to coat the squid well in the flour mixture.

5 Heat about 2 inches of peanut oil in a large preheated wok.

6 Add the squid pieces to the wok and stir-fry, in batches, for about 2 minutes, or until the squid pieces start to curl up. Do not overcook or the squid will become tough.

7 Remove the squid pieces with a slotted spoon, transfer to absorbent paper towels, and drain thoroughly.

8 Transfer to serving plates and serve immediately with a dipping sauce.

COOK'S TIP

Squid tubes may be purchased frozen if they are not available fresh. They are usually ready-cleaned and are easy to use. Ensure that they are completely thawed before cooking.

Stir-Fried Squid with Green Bell Peppers & Black Bean Sauce

Squid really is wonderful if quickly cooked, as in this recipe, and contrary to popular belief it is not tough and rubbery unless it is overcooked.

Serves 4

INGREDIENTS

1 pound squid rings
2 tbsp all-purpose flour
$^{1}/_{2}$ tsp salt

1 green bell pepper
2 tbsp peanut oil
1 red onion, sliced

5$^{3}/_{4}$ ounce jar black bean sauce

1 Rinse the squid rings under cold running water and pat dry with absorbent paper towels.

2 Place the all-purpose flour and salt in a bowl and mix together. Add the squid rings and toss until they are finely coated.

3 Using a sharp knife, seed the bell pepper. Slice the bell pepper into thin strips.

4 Heat the peanut oil in a large preheated wok.

5 Add the bell pepper and red onion to the wok and stir-fry for about 2 minutes, or until the vegetables are just beginning to soften.

6 Add the squid rings to the wok and cook for a further 5 minutes, or until the squid is cooked through.

7 Add the black bean sauce to the wok and heat through until the juices are bubbling. Transfer to warm serving bowls and serve immediately.

COOK'S TIP

Serve this recipe with fried rice or noodles tossed in soy sauce, if you wish.

Vegetarian Dishes

As vegetables are so plentiful and diverse in the Far East, they play a major role in the diet. Other ingredients, such as bean curd, are added to the vegetarian diet, which is both a healthy and economical choice. Bean curd is produced from the soy bean, which is grown in abundance in these countries.
The cake variety of bean curd is frequently used in stir-frying for texture and it is perfect for absorbing all of the component flavors of the dish.

The wok is perfect for cooking vegetables, as it cooks them very quickly which helps to retain nutrients and crispness, and thus produces a range of colorful and flavorful recipes. Some of the dishes contained in this chapter are ideal accompaniments, while others, such as vegetable curries, are combined with spices to produce more substantial main meals.

The following chapter shows the wonderful versatility of vegetables and contains something for everyone, which should delight vegetarians and meat-eaters alike.

Stir-Fried Japanese Mushroom Noodles

*This quick dish is an ideal lunchtime meal, packed
with mixed mushrooms in a sweet sauce.*

Serves 4

INGREDIENTS

9 ounces Japanese egg noodles
2 tbsp sunflower oil
1 red onion, sliced
1 clove garlic, crushed

1 pound mixed mushrooms (shiitake,
  oyster, brown cap)
12 ounces bok choy (or Chinese
  cabbage)

2 tbsp sweet sherry
6 tbsp soy sauce
4 scallions, sliced
1 tbsp toasted sesame seeds

1 Place the Japanese egg noodles in a large bowl. Pour over enough boiling water to cover, and set aside to soak for 10 minutes.

2 Heat the sunflower oil in a large preheated wok.

3 Add the red onion and garlic to the wok and stir-fry for 2–3 minutes, or until softened.

4 Add the mushrooms to the wok and stir-fry for about 5 minutes, or until the mushrooms have softened.

5 Drain the egg noodles thoroughly.

6 Add the the bok choy (or Chinese cabbage), noodles, sweet sherry, and soy sauce to the wok. Toss all of the ingredients together and stir-fry for 2–3 minutes or until the liquid is just bubbling.

7 Transfer the mushroom noodles to warm serving bowls and scatter with sliced scallions and toasted sesame seeds. Serve the stir-fried noodles immediately.

COOK'S TIP

The variety of mushrooms in supermarkets has greatly improved and a good mixture should be easily obtainable. If not, use the more common button and flat mushrooms.

Stir-Fried Vegetables with Sherry & Soy Sauce

This is a simple, yet tasty side dish which is just as delicious as a snack or main course.

Serves 4

INGREDIENTS

2 tbsp sunflower oil
1 red onion, sliced
3–4 medium carrots, thinly sliced
6 ounces zucchini, sliced diagonally
1 red bell pepper, seeded and sliced
1 small head Chinese
   cabbage, shredded

$^3/_4$ cup bean sprouts
8 ounce can bamboo shoots, drained
$^1/_4$ cup cashew nuts, toasted

SAUCE:
3 tbsp medium sherry
3 tbsp light soy sauce

1 tsp ground ginger
1 clove garlic, crushed
1 tsp cornstarch
1 tbsp tomato paste

1 Heat the sunflower oil in a large preheated wok.

2 Add the red onion slices to the wok and stir-fry for 2–3 minutes, or until just beginning to soften.

3 Add the carrots, zucchini, and bell pepper slices to the wok and stir-fry for a further 5 minutes.

4 Add the Chinese cabbage, bean sprouts, and bamboo shoots to the wok and heat through for 2–3 minutes, or until the leaves just begin to wilt.

5 Scatter the cashew nuts over the top of the vegetables.

6 Mix together the sherry, soy sauce, ginger, garlic, cornstarch, and tomato paste.

7 Pour the mixture over the vegetables and toss well. Simmer gently for 2–3 minutes, or until the juices start to thicken. Serve immediately.

COOK'S TIP

Use any mixture of fresh vegetables that you have to hand in this very versatile dish.

Stir-Fried Bok Choy with Red Onion & Cashew Nuts

Plum sauce is readily available in jars and has a terrific, sweet flavor which complements the vegetables.

Serves 4

INGREDIENTS

2 tbsp peanut oil
2 red onions, cut into thin wedges

6 ounces red cabbage, thinly shredded
8 ounces bok choy

2 tbsp plum sauce
1 cup roasted cashew nuts

1 Heat the peanut oil in a large preheated wok.

2 Add the onion wedges to the wok and stir-fry for about 5 minutes, or until the onions are just beginning to brown.

3 Add the red cabbage to the wok and stir-fry for a further 2–3 minutes.

4 Add the bok choy to the wok and stir-fry for about 5 minutes, or until the leaves have wilted.

5 Drizzle the plum sauce over the vegetables, toss together until well combined, and heat until the liquid is bubbling.

6 Scatter with the roasted cashew nuts and transfer to warm serving bowls. Serve immediately.

COOK'S TIP

Plum sauce has a unique, fruity flavor—a sweet and sour with a difference.

VARIATION

Use unsalted peanuts instead of the cashew nuts, if desired.

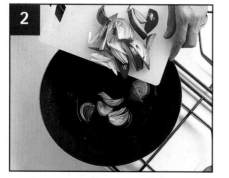

Bean Curd with Soy Sauce, Green Bell Peppers, & Crispy Onions

Bean curd is perfect for marinating, as it readily absorbs flavors for a great tasting main dish.

Serves 4

INGREDIENTS

12 ounces bean curd
2 cloves garlic, crushed
4 tbsp soy sauce

1 tbsp sweet chili sauce
6 tbsp sunflower oil
1 onion, sliced

1 green bell pepper, seeded and diced
1 tbsp sesame oil

1 Drain the bean curd and, using a sharp knife, cut it into bite-size pieces. Place the bean curd pieces in a shallow nonmetallic dish.

2 Mix together the garlic, soy sauce, and sweet chili sauce and drizzle over the bean curd. Toss well to coat each piece and set aside to marinate for about 20 minutes.

3 Meanwhile, heat the sunflower oil in a large preheated wok.

4 Add the onion slices to the wok and stir-fry over a high heat until they brown and become crispy. Remove the onion slices with a slotted spoon and drain on absorbent kitchen paper.

5 Add the bean curd to the hot oil and stir-fry for about 5 minutes.

6 Remove all but 1 tablespoon of the oil from the wok. Add the bell pepper to the wok and stir-fry for 2–3 minutes, or until it has softened.

7 Return the bean curd and onions to the wok and heat through, stirring occasionally. Drizzle with the sesame oil.

8 Transfer to serving plates and serve immediately.

COOK'S TIP

If you are in a real hurry, buy ready-marinated bean curd from your supermarket.

Stir-Fried Green Beans with Lettuce & Black Bean Sauce

*A terrific side dish, the variety of greens in this recipe
makes it as attractive as it is tasty.*

Serves 4

INGREDIENTS

1 tsp chili oil
2 tbsp butter
1^{1}/$_{2}$ cups fine green beans, sliced
4 shallots, sliced

1 clove garlic, crushed
3^{1}/$_{2}$ ounces shiitake mushrooms,
  thinly sliced
1 iceberg lettuce, shredded

4 tbsp black bean sauce

1 Heat the chili oil and butter in a large preheated wok.

2 Add the green beans, shallots, garlic, and mushrooms to the wok and stir-fry for 2–3 minutes.

3 Add the shredded lettuce to the wok and stir-fry until the leaves have wilted.

4 Stir the black bean sauce into the mixture in the wok and heat through, tossing to mix, until the sauce is bubbling. Serve.

COOK'S TIP

To make your own black bean sauce, soak ^{1}/$_{3}$ cup dried black beans overnight in cold water. Drain and place in a pan of cold water, boil for 10 minutes, then drain. Return the beans to the pan with 2 cups vegetable stock and boil. Blend 1 tablespoon each of malt vinegar, soy sauce, sugar, 1^{1}/$_{2}$ teaspoons cornstarch, 1 chopped red chili, and ^{1}/$_{2}$ inch ginger root. Add to the pan and simmer for 40 minutes.

COOK'S TIP

If possible, use Chinese green beans, which are tender and can be eaten whole. They are available from specialty Chinese stores.

Deep-fried Zucchini

These zucchini fritters are irresistible and could be served as a starter or snack with a chili dip.

Serves 4

INGREDIENTS

1 pound zucchini
1 egg white

$^1/_3$ cup cornstarch
1 tsp salt

1 tsp Chinese five-spice powder
oil, for deep-frying

---

1 Using a sharp knife, slice the zucchini into rings or sticks.

2 Place the egg white in a small mixing bowl. Lightly beat the egg white until foamy, using a fork.

3 Mix the cornstarch, salt and five-spice powder and sprinkle onto a large plate.

4 Heat the oil for deep-frying in a large preheated wok.

5 Dip each piece of zucchini into the beaten egg white then coat in the cornstarch mixture.

6 Deep-fry the zucchini, in batches, for about 5 minutes or until pale golden and crispy. Repeat with the remaining zucchini slices or sticks.

7 Remove the zucchini with a slotted spoon and drain on absorbent kitchen paper while you deep-fry the remainder.

8 Transfer the zucchini to warm serving plates and serve immediately.

VARIATION

Alter the seasoning by using chili powder or curry powder instead of the Chinese five-spice powder, if desired.

Deep-fried Chili Corn Balls

These small corn balls have a wonderful hot and sweet flavor, offset
by the pungent cilantro for a real taste of Thailand.

Serves 4

INGREDIENTS

6 scallions, sliced
3 tbsp fresh cilantro, chopped
8 ounces canned corn
1 tsp mild chili powder

1 tbsp sweet chili sauce
1/4 cup shredded coconut
1 egg
1/3 cup cornmeal

oil, for deep-frying
extra sweet chili sauce, to serve

1 In a large mixing bowl, mix together the scallions, cilantro, corn, chili powder, chili sauce, coconut, egg, and cornmeal. Cover and let stand for about 10 minutes.

2 Heat the oil for deep-frying in a large preheated wok.

3 Carefully drop spoonfuls of the chili and cornmeal mixture into the hot oil. Deep-fry the chill corn balls, in batches, for 4–5 minutes or until crispy and a deep golden brown color.

4 Remove the chili corn balls with a slotted spoon, transfer to paper towels and let drain thoroughly.

5 Transfer to serving plates and serve with an extra sweet chili sauce for dipping.

COOK'S TIP

For safe deep-frying in a round-bottomed wok, place it on a wok rack so that it rests securely. Only half-fill the wok with oil. Never leave the wok unattended over a high heat.

COOK'S TIP

Cornmeal is a type of meal ground from corn or maize. It is available in most large supermarkets or in healthfood shops.

Asparagus & Red Bell Pepper Packets

These small packets are ideal as part of a main meal and irresistible
as a quick snack with extra plum sauce for dipping.

Serves 4

INGREDIENTS

3¹/₂ ounces fine tip asparagus
1 red bell pepper, seeded and
    thinly sliced

¹/₄ cup bean sprouts
2 tbsp plum sauce
8 sheets filo pastry

1 egg yolk, beaten
oil, for deep-frying

1 Place the asparagus, bell pepper, and bean sprouts in a large mixing bowl.

2 Add the plum sauce to the vegetables and mix until well combined.

3 Spread out the sheets of filo pastry on a clean counter or chopping board.

4 Place a little of the asparagus and red bell pepper filling at the top end of each filo pastry sheet. Brush the edges of the filo pastry with a little of the beaten egg yolk.

5 Roll up the filo pastry, tucking in the ends and enclosing the filling like a spring roll.

6 Heat the oil for deep-frying in a large preheated wok.

7 Carefully cook the packets, 2 at a time, in the hot oil for 4–5 minutes, or until crispy.

8 Remove the packets with a slotted spoon and drain on absorbent paper towels.

9 Transfer the packets to individual warm serving plates and serve immediately.

COOK'S TIP

Be sure to use fine-tipped asparagus, as it is more tender than the larger stems.

Carrot & Orange Stir-Fry

*Carrots and oranges have long been combined in Southeast Asian cooking,
the orange juice bringing out the sweetness of the carrots.*

Serves 4

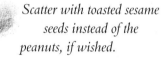
INGREDIENTS

2 tbsp sunflower oil	2 oranges, peeled and segmented	2 tbsp light soy
1 pound carrots, grated	2 tbsp tomato ketchup	1 cup chopped peanuts
8 ounces leeks, shredded	1 tbsp sugar	

1 Heat the sunflower oil in a large preheated wok.

2 Add the grated carrot and leeks to the wok and stir-fry for 2–3 minutes, or until the vegetables have just softened.

3 Add the orange segments to the wok and heat through gently, ensuring that you do not break up the orange segments as you stir the mixture.

4 Mix the tomato ketchup, sugar and soy sauce together in a small bowl.

5 Add the tomato and sugar mixture to the wok and stir-fry for a further 2 minutes.

6 Transfer the stir-fry to warm serving bowls and scatter with the chopped peanuts. Serve immediately.

VARIATION

You could use pineapple instead of orange, if wished. If using canned pineapple, make sure that it is in natural juice not syrup, as it will spoil the fresh taste of this dish.

VARIATION

Scatter with toasted sesame seeds instead of the peanuts, if wished.

Spinach Stir-Fry with Shiitake & Honey

This stir-fry is the perfect accompaniment to fish or bean curd dishes, and it is so quick and simple to make.

Serves 4

INGREDIENTS

3 tbsp peanut oil

12 ounces shiitake mushrooms, sliced

2 cloves garlic, crushed

12 ounces baby leaf spinach

2 tbsp dry sherry

2 tbsp clear honey

4 scallions, sliced

1 Heat the peanut oil in a large preheated wok.

2 Add the shiitake mushrooms to the wok and stir-fry for about 5 minutes, or until the mushrooms have softened.

3 Add the crushed garlic and baby leaf spinach to the mushrooms in the wok and stir-fry for a further 2–3 minutes, or until the spinach leaves have just begun to wilt.

4 Mix together the dry sherry and clear honey in a small bowl until well combined.

5 Drizzle the sherry and honey mixture over the spinach and heat through.

6 Transfer the stir-fry to warm serving dishes and scatter with scallion slices. Serve immediately, while hot.

COOK'S TIP

A good quality, dry pale sherry should be used in this recipe. Cream or sweet sherry should not be substituted. Rice wine is often used in Chinese cooking, but sherry can be used instead.

COOK'S TIP

Nutmeg complements the flavor of spinach and it is a classic combination. Add a pinch of nutmeg to the dish in step 3, if you wish.

Chinese Vegetable Rice

This rice can either be served as a meal in itself or as an accompaniment to other vegetable recipes.

Serves 4

INGREDIENTS

$1^3/_4$ cups long grain white rice
1 tsp ground turmeric
2 tbsp sunflower oil
8 ounces zucchini, sliced
1 red bell pepper, seeded
  and sliced

1 green bell pepper, seeded
  and sliced
1 green chili, seeded and
  finely chopped
1 medium carrot, coarsely grated
$^3/_4$ cup bean sprouts

6 scallions, sliced, plus extra to
  garnish
2 tbsp soy sauce
salt

1 Place the rice and ground turmeric in a large saucepan of lightly salted water and bring to a boil. Reduce the heat and simmer until the rice is just tender. Drain the rice thoroughly and press out any excess water with a sheet of double thickness paper towels.

2 Heat the sunflower oil in a large preheated wok.

3 Add the zucchini to the wok and stir-fry for about 2 minutes.

4 Add the bell peppers and chili to the wok and stir-fry for 2–3 minutes.

5 Add the cooked rice to the mixture in the wok, a little at a time, tossing well after each addition.

6 Add the carrots, bean sprouts, and scallions to the wok and stir-fry for a further 2 minutes. Drizzle the Chinese vegetable rice with soy sauce and serve at once, garnished with extra scallions, if desired.

VARIATION

For real luxury, add a few saffron strands infused in boiling water instead of the turmeric.

Vegetable Stir-Fry with Hoisin Sauce

This vegetable stir-fry has rice added to it and it can be served as a meal in itself.

Serves 4

INGREDIENTS

2 tbsp sunflower oil
1 red onion, sliced
1–2 medium carrots, sliced

1 yellow bell pepper, seeded
  and diced
1 cup cooked brown rice
6 ounces snow peas

³/4 cup bean sprouts
4 tbsp hoisin sauce
1 tbsp snipped fresh chives

1 Heat the sunflower oil in a large preheated wok.

2 Add the red onion slices, carrots, and yellow bell pepper to the wok and stir-fry for about 3 minutes.

3 Add the cooked brown rice, snow peas, sliced diagonally, if wished, and bean sprouts to the mixture in the wok and stir-fry for a further 2 minutes.

4 Stir the hoisin sauce into the vegetables and mix until well combined and completely heated through.

5 Transfer to warm serving dishes and scatter with the snipped fresh chives. Serve immediately.

VARIATION

Almost any vegetables could be used in this dish: other good choices would be broccoli flowerets, baby corn cobs, green peas, Chinese cabbage, and young spinach leaves. Either white or black (oyster) mushrooms can also be used to give a greater diversity of textures. In addition, make sure that there is a good variety of color in this dish.

COOK'S TIP

Hoisin sauce is a dark brown, reddish sauce made from soy beans, garlic, chili, and various other spices, and is commonly used in Chinese cookery. It may also be used as a dipping sauce.

Sweet & Sour Cauliflower & Cilantro Stir-Fry

Although sweet and sour flavorings are mainly associated with pork, they are ideal for flavoring vegetables, as in this tasty recipe.

Serves 4

INGREDIENTS

1 pound cauliflower flowerets

2 tbsp sunflower oil

1 onion, sliced

3–4 medium carrots, sliced

$3^1/2$ ounces snow peas

1 ripe mango, sliced

$^1/2$ cup bean sprouts

3 tbsp chopped fresh cilantro

3 tbsp fresh lime juice

1 tbsp clear honey

6 tbsp coconut milk

salt

---

1 Bring a large saucepan of lightly salted water to a boil. Lower the heat slightly, add the cauliflower flowerets to the pan and cook for about 2 minutes. Remove from the heat and drain the cauliflower thoroughly in a colander.

2 Heat the sunflower oil in a large preheated wok.

3 Add the onion and carrots to the wok and stir-fry for about 5 minutes.

4 Add the drained cauliflower and snow peas to the wok and stir-fry for 2–3 minutes.

5 Add the mango and bean sprouts to the wok and stir-fry for about 2 minutes.

6 Mix together the cilantro, lime juice, honey, and coconut milk in a bowl.

7 Add the cilantro mixture and stir-fry for about 2 minutes or until the juices are bubbling.

8 Transfer the stir-fry to serving dishes and serve immediately.

VARIATION

Use broccoli instead of the cauliflower as an alternative, if wished.

Broccoli & Chinese Cabbage with Black Bean Sauce

*Broccoli works well with the black bean sauce in this recipe,
while the almonds add extra crunch and flavor.*

Serves 4

INGREDIENTS

1 pound broccoli flowerets
2 tbsp sunflower oil
1 onion, sliced

2 cloves garlic, thinly sliced
1/4 cup slivered almonds
1 head Chinese cabbage, shredded

4 tbsp black bean sauce

1 Bring a large saucepan of water to a boil. Add the broccoli flowerets to the pan and cook for 1 minute. Drain the broccoli thoroughly.

2 Meanwhile, heat the sunflower oil in a large preheated wok.

3 Add the onion and garlic to the wok and stir-fry until just beginning to brown.

4 Add the drained broccoli flowerets and the flaked almonds to the mixture in the wok and stir-fry for a further 2–3 minutes.

5 Add the Chinese cabbage to the wok and stir-fry for a further 2 minutes.

6 Stir the black bean sauce into the vegetables in the wok, tossing to mix, and cook until the juices are just beginning to bubble.

7 Transfer the vegetables to warm serving bowls and serve immediately.

VARIATION

Use unsalted cashew nuts instead of the almonds, if wished.

Chinese Mushrooms with Deep-fried Bean Curd

Chinese mushrooms are available from Chinese supermarkets and healthfood shops and add a unique flavor to Asian dishes.

Serves 4

INGREDIENTS

1 ounce dried Chinese mushrooms
1 pound bean curd
4 tbsp cornstarch

oil, for deep-frying
2 cloves garlic, finely chopped
1-inch piece of ginger root, grated

1 cup frozen or fresh peas

1 Place the Chinese mushrooms in a large bowl. Pour in enough boiling water to cover and let stand for about 10 minutes.

2 Meanwhile, cut the bean curd into bite-size cubes, using a sharp knife.

3 Place the cornstarch in a medium-size bowl.

4 Toss the bean curd in the cornstarch until thoroughly and evenly coated.

5 Heat the oil for deep-frying in a large preheated wok.

6 Add the cubes of bean curd to the wok and deep-fry, in batches, for 2–3 minutes, or until golden and crispy. Remove the bean curd with a slotted spoon and let drain on absorbent paper towels.

7 Drain off all but 2 tablespoons of oil from the wok. Add the garlic, ginger, and Chinese mushrooms to the wok and stir-fry for 2–3 minutes.

8 Return the cooked bean curd to the wok and add the peas. Heat through for 1 minute, then serve hot.

COOK'S TIP

Use marinated bean curd for extra flavor.

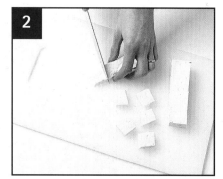

Stir-Fried Butternut Squash with Cashew Nuts & Cilantro

Butternut squash is, as its name suggests, deliciously buttery and nutty in flavor. If the squash is not in season, use sweet potatoes instead.

Serves 4

INGREDIENTS

2 1/4 pounds butternut squash, peeled
3 tbsp peanut oil
1 onion, sliced
2 cloves garlic, crushed
1 tsp coriander seeds

1 tsp cumin seeds
2 tbsp chopped cilantro
2/3 cup coconut milk
1/2 cup water
1 cup salted cashew nuts

TO GARNISH:
freshly grated lime zest
fresh cilantro
lime wedges

1 Using a sharp knife, slice the butternut squash into small, bite-size cubes.

2 Heat the peanut oil in a large preheated wok.

3 Add the squash, onion, and garlic to the wok and stir-fry for 5 minutes.

4 Stir in the coriander seeds, cumin, and fresh cilantro and stir-fry for 1 minute.

5 Add the coconut milk and water to the wok and bring to a boil. Cover the wok and simmer for 10–15 minutes, or until the squash is tender.

6 Add the cashew nuts and stir to combine.

7 Transfer to warm serving dishes and garnish with freshly grated lime zest, fresh cilantro, and wedges of lime Serve hot.

COOK'S TIP

If you do not have coconut milk, grate some creamed coconut into the dish with the water in step 5.

Quorn with Ginger & Mixed Vegetables

Quorn, also known as mycoprotein, absorbs all of the flavors in a dish, making it ideal for this recipe which is packed with classic Chinese flavorings.

Serves 4

INGREDIENTS

1 tbsp grated fresh ginger root	1 clove garlic, crushed	³/₄ cup green beans, sliced
1 tsp ground ginger	2 tbsp soy sauce	4 stalks celery, sliced
1 tbsp tomato paste	12 ounces Quorn or	1 red bell pepper, seeded and sliced
2 tbsp sunflower oil	mycoprotein cubes	boiled rice, to serve
	3–4 medium carrots, sliced	

1 Place the grated fresh ginger, ground ginger, tomato paste, 1 tablespoon of the sunflower oil, garlic, soy sauce, and Quorn or mycoprotein in a large bowl. Mix well to combine, stirring carefully so that you don't break up the Quorn or mycoprotein. Cover and marinate for 20 minutes.

2 Heat the remaining sunflower oil in a large preheated wok.

3 Add the marinated Quorn mixture to the wok and stir-fry for about 2 minutes.

4 Add the carrots, green beans, celery, and red bell pepper to the wok and stir-fry for a further 5 minutes.

5 Transfer the stir-fry to warm serving dishes and serve immediately with freshly cooked boiled rice.

COOK'S TIP

Ginger root will keep for several weeks in a cool, dry place. Ginger root can also be kept frozen—break off lumps as needed.

VARIATION

Use bean curd instead of the Quorn, if you prefer.

Leeks with Baby Corn Cobs & Yellow Bean Sauce

This is a simple side dish which is ideal with other main meal vegetarian or fish dishes.

Serves 4

INGREDIENTS

3 tbsp peanut oil	8 ounces Chinese cabbage, shredded	6 scallions, sliced
1 pound leeks, sliced	6 ounces baby corn cobs, halved	4 tbsp yellow bean sauce

1 Heat the peanut oil in a large preheated wok.

2 Add the leeks, shredded Chinese cabbage, and baby corn cobs to the wok and stir-fry over a high heat for about 5 minutes, or until the edges of the vegetables are beginning to brown slightly.

3 Add the scallions to the wok, stirring to combine.

4 Add the yellow bean sauce to the mixture in the wok and stir-fry for a further 2 minutes, or until heated through.

5 Transfer to warm serving dishes and serve immediately.

COOK'S TIP

Yellow bean sauce adds an authentic Chinese flavor to stir-fries. It is made from crushed salted soy beans mixed with flour and spices to make a thick paste. It is mild in flavor and is excellent with chicken, vegetables, and fish.

COOK'S TIP

Baby corn cobs are sweeter and have a more delicate flavor than the larger corn cobs and are therefore perfect for stir-frying.

Vegetable Stir-Fry

A range of delicious flavors is captured in this simple recipe which is ideal if you are in a hurry.

Serves 4

INGREDIENTS

3 tbsp olive oil
8 baby onions, halved
1 eggplant, cubed
8 ounces zucchini, sliced

8 ounces open-cap mushrooms, halved
2 cloves garlic, crushed
14 ounce can chopped tomatoes
2 tbsp sun-dried tomato paste

freshly ground black pepper
fresh basil leaves, to garnish

1 Heat the olive oil in a large preheated wok.

2 Add the baby onions and eggplant to the wok and stir-fry for 5 minutes, or until the vegetables are golden and just beginning to soften.

3 Add the zucchini, mushrooms, garlic, tomatoes, and tomato paste to the wok and stir-fry for about 5 minutes. Reduce the heat and simmer for 10 minutes, or until the vegetables are tender.

4 Season with freshly ground black pepper and scatter with fresh basil leaves. Serve immediately.

COOK'S TIP

Wok cooking is an excellent means of cooking for vegetarians as it is a quick and easy way of serving up delicious dishes of crisp, tasty vegetables. All ingredients should be cut into uniform sizes with as many cut surfaces exposed as possible for quick cooking.

VARIATION

If you want to serve this as a vegetarian main meal, add cubed bean curd in step 3.

Stir-Fried Bell Pepper Trio with Chestnuts & Garlic

*This a crisp and colorful recipe, topped with crisp,
shredded leeks for both flavor and color.*

Serves 4

INGREDIENTS

8 ounces leeks	1 green bell pepper, seeded and diced	2 cloves garlic, crushed
oil, for deep-frying	1 red bell pepper, seeded and diced	3 tbsp light soy sauce
3 tbsp peanut oil	7 ounce can water chestnuts, drained	
1 yellow bell pepper, seeded and diced	and sliced	

1 To make the garnish, finely slice the leeks into thin strips, using a sharp knife.

2 Heat the oil for deep-frying in a wok and cook the leeks for 2–3 minute, or until crispy. Set the crispy leeks aside until they are required.

3 Heat the 3 tablespoons of peanut oil in the wok.

4 Add the bell peppers to the wok and stir-fry over a high heat for about 5 minutes, or until they are just beginning to brown at the edges and to soften.

5 Add the sliced water chestnuts, garlic, and light soy sauce to the wok and stir-fry all of the vegetables for a further 2–3 minutes.

6 Spoon the bell pepper stir-fry onto warm serving plates.

7 Garnish the stir-fry with the crispy leeks and serve.

VARIATION

Add 1 tbsp of hoisin sauce with the soy sauce in step 5 for extra flavor and spice.

Spiced Eggplant Stir-Fry

This is a spicy and sweet dish, flavored with mango chutney and heated up with chilies for a really wonderful combination of flavors.

Serves 4

INGREDIENTS

3 tbsp peanut oil
2 onions, sliced
2 cloves garlic, chopped
2 eggplants, diced

2 red chilies, seeded and very
  finely chopped
2 tbsp sugar
6 scallions, sliced

3 tbsp mango chutney
oil, for deep-frying
2 cloves garlic, sliced, to garnish

1 Heat the peanut oil in a large preheated wok.

2 Add the onions and chopped garlic to the wok, stirring well.

3 Add the eggplants and chilies to the wok and stir-fry for 5 minutes.

4 Add the sugar, scallions, and mango chutney to the wok, stirring well. Reduce the heat slightly, cover, and simmer, stirring from time to time, for about 15 minutes or until the eggplants are tender.

5 Transfer the stir-fry to warm serving bowls and keep warm. Heat the oil for deep-frying in the wok and quickly stir-fry the slices of garlic. Garnish the bowls of stir-fry with the deep-fried garlic and serve immediately.

COOK'S TIP

The "hotness" of chilies varies enormously, so always use with caution, but as a general guide the smaller they are the hotter they will be. The seeds are the hottest part and so are usually discarded.

COOK'S TIP

Keep the vegetables moving around the wok as the eggplant will soak up the oil very quickly and may begin to burn if left unattended.

Stir-Fried Vegetables with Peanuts & Eggs

Known as Gado Gado in China, this is a true classic which never fades from popularity.
A delicious warm salad with a peanut sauce.

Serves 4

INGREDIENTS

2 eggs
3–4 medium carrots
12 ounces white cabbage

2 tbsp vegetable oil
1 red bell pepper, seeded and
    thinly sliced
$^3/_4$ cup bean sprouts

1 tbsp tomato ketchup
2 tbsp soy sauce
$^1/_3$ cup salted peanuts, chopped

1 Bring a small saucepan of water to a boil. Add the eggs to the pan and cook for about 7 minutes. Remove the eggs from the pan and cool under cold running water for 1 minute.

2 Carefully peel the shells from the eggs and then cut the eggs into quarters.

3 Peel and coarsely grate the carrots.

4 Using a sharp knife, thinly shred the white cabbage.

5 Heat the vegetable oil in a large preheated wok.

6 Add the carrots, white cabbage, and bell pepper to the wok and stir-fry for 3 minutes.

7 Add the bean sprouts to the wok and stir-fry for 2 minutes.

8 Add the tomato ketchup, soy sauce, and peanuts to the wok and stir-fry for 1 minute.

9 Transfer the stir-fry to warm serving plates and garnish

with the hard-cooked)egg quarters. Serve immediately.

COOK'S TIP

The eggs are cooled in cold water immediately after cooking in order to prevent the egg yolk blackening around the edges.

Rice & Noodles

Rice and noodles are staples in Asia, as they are cheap, plentiful, nutritious, and delicious. They are such versatile ingredients and are therefore always served as part of a meal. Many rice and noodle dishes are served as accompaniments and others as main dishes with meat, vegetables, and fish flavored with spices and seasonings.

There are several types of rice grown and used in China and the various Asian countries, each perfect for its specific use. Owing to the climates of these countries and the perfect rice-growing conditions, natives have adapted recipes to suit their own individual tastes. Plain rice is served to punctuate a meal and settle the stomach during larger meals.

Noodles vary from country to country and are eaten day and night in various forms. Thin egg noodles are made from wheat flour, water, and egg and are probably the most common in the Western diet. They are available both fresh and dried and require very little cooking. Rice noodles are also widely used, known as sha he in China and harusame in Japan. Mung beans are also ground to produce cellophane or transparent noodles which are perfect for reheating and adding to recipes.

Fried Rice with Spicy Beans

This rice is really colorful and crunchy with the addition of corn and red kidney beans.
It may be served as a main vegetarian dish or as a side dish with meat or fish.

Serves 4

INGREDIENTS

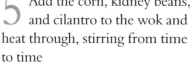

3 tbsp sunflower oil
1 onion, finely chopped
1 cup long grain white rice

1 green bell pepper, seeded and diced
1 tsp chili powder
$2^{1}/_{2}$ cups boiling water

$^{1}/_{2}$ cup canned corn
8 ounces canned red kidney beans
2 tbsp chopped fresh cilantro

1 Heat the sunflower oil in a large preheated wok.

2 Add the finely chopped onion to the wok and stir-fry for about 2 minutes, or until the onion has softened.

3 Add the long grain rice, diced bell pepper, and chili powder to the wok and stir-fry for 1 minute.

4 Pour $2^{1}/_{2}$ cups of boiling water into the wok. Bring to a boil, then reduce the heat, and simmer the mixture for about 15 minutes.

5 Add the corn, kidney beans, and cilantro to the wok and heat through, stirring from time to time

6 Transfer to a serving bowl and serve hot, scattered with extra cilantro, if wished.

COOK'S TIP

For perfect fried rice, the raw rice should ideally be soaked in a bowl of water for a short time before cooking to remove excess starch. Short grain Asian rice can be substituted for the long grain rice.

VARIATION

For extra heat, add 1 chopped fresh red chilli as well as the chilli powder in step 3.

Coconut Rice

This fragrant, sweet rice is delicious served with meat,
vegetable, or fish dishes as part of a Thai menu.

Serves 4

INGREDIENTS

$1^1/_3$ cups long grain white rice
$2^1/_2$ cups water

$^1/_2$ tsp salt
$^1/_3$ cup coconut milk

$^1/_4$ cup shredded coconut

1 Rinse the rice thoroughly under cold running water until the water runs clear.

2 Drain the rice thoroughly in a strainer.

3 Place the rice in a wok with $2^1/_2$ cups water.

4 Add the salt and coconut milk to the wok and bring to a boil. Cover the wok, reduce the heat, and simmer for 10 minutes.

5 Remove the lid from the wok and fluff up the rice with a fork—all of the liquid should be absorbed and the rice grains should be tender.

6 Spoon the coconut rice into a warm serving bowl and scatter with the shredded coconut. Transfer to a serving dish and serve immediately.

COOK'S TIP

Coconut milk is not the liquid found inside coconuts—that is called coconut water. Coconut milk is made from the white coconut flesh soaked in water and milk and then squeezed to extract all of the flavor. You can make your own or buy it in cans.

COOK'S TIP

The rice is rinsed under cold running water to remove some of the starch and to prevent the grains from sticking together.

Stir-fried Onion Rice with Five-spice Chicken

This dish has a wonderful color obtained from the turmeric, and a great spicy flavor, making it very appealing all round.

Serves 4

INGREDIENTS

1 tbsp Chinese five-spice powder
2 tbsp cornstarch
12 ounces boneless, skinless chicken
  breasts, cubed

3 tbsp peanut oil
1 onion, diced
1 cup long grain white rice
$1/2$ tsp turmeric

$2^1/2$ cups chicken stock
2 tbsp snipped fresh chives

1 Place the Chinese five-spice powder and cornstarch in a large bowl. Add the chicken pieces and toss to coat all over.

2 Heat 2 tablespoons of the peanut oil in a large preheated wok. Add the chicken pieces to the wok and stir-fry for 5 minutes. Using a slotted spoon, remove the chicken and set aside.

3 Add the remaining peanut oil to the wok. Heat until hot, then reduce the heat.

4 Add the onion to the wok and stir-fry for 1 minute.

5 Add the rice, turmeric, and chicken stock to the wok and bring to a boil.

6 Return the chicken pieces to the wok, reduce the heat, and simmer for 10 minutes, or until the liquid has been absorbed and the rice is tender.

7 Add the chives, stir to mix and serve hot.

COOK'S TIP

Be careful when using turmeric, as it can stain the hands and clothes a distinctive shade of yellow.

Chinese Chicken Rice

This is a really colorful main meal or side dish,
which tastes just as good as it looks.

Serves 4

INGREDIENTS

1³/4 cups long grain white rice
1 tsp turmeric
2 tbsp sunflower oil
12 ounces skinless, boneless chicken
  breasts or thighs, sliced

1 red bell pepper, seeded and sliced
1 green bell pepper, seeded and sliced
1 green chili, seeded and
  finely chopped
1 medium carrot, coarsely grated

³/4 cup bean sprouts
6 scallions, sliced, plus extra to
  garnish
2 tbsp soy sauce
salt

1 Place the rice and turmeric in a large saucepan of lightly salted water and cook until the grains of rice are just tender, about 10 minutes. Drain the rice thoroughly and press out any excess water with a double thickness of paper towels.

2 Heat the sunflower oil in a large preheated wok.

3 Add the strips of chicken to the wok and stir-fry over a high heat until the chicken is just beginning to turn a golden color.

4 Add the bell peppers and chili to the wok and stir-fry for 2–3 minutes.

5 Add the rice to the wok, a little at a time, tossing well after each addition, until well combined.

6 Add the carrot, bean sprouts, and scallions to the mixture in the wok and stir-fry for a further 2 minutes.

7 Drizzle with the soy sauce and mix well.

8 Garnish with extra scallions, if wished, and serve at once.

VARIATION

Use pork marinated in hoisin
sauce instead of the chicken,
if wished.

Sweet Chili Pork Fried Rice

This is a variation of egg fried rice which may be served
as an accompaniment to a main meal dish.

Serves 4

INGREDIENTS

1 pound pork tenderloin
2 tbsp sunflower oil
2 tbsp sweet chili sauce, plus extra
   to serve
1 onion, sliced

2–3 medium carrots, cut into
   thin sticks
6 ounces zucchini, cut into sticks
1 cup canned bamboo shoots,
   drained and rinsed

4³/4 cups cooked long grain rice
1 egg, beaten
1 tbsp chopped fresh parsley

1 Using a sharp knife, slice the pork thinly.

2 Heat the sunflower oil in a large preheated wok.

3 Add the pork to the wok and stir-fry for 5 minutes.

4 Add the chili sauce to the wok and allow to bubble, stirring, for 2–3 minutes, or until syrupy.

5 Add the onions, carrots, zucchini, and bamboo shoots to the wok and stir-fry for a further 3 minutes.

6 Add the cooked rice and stir-fry for 2–3 minutes, or until the rice is heated through.

7 Drizzle the beaten egg over the top of the fried rice and cook, tossing the ingredients in the wok, until the egg sets.

8 Scatter with chopped fresh parsley and serve immediately, with extra sweet chili sauce, if desired.

COOK'S TIP

For a really quick dish, add frozen mixed vegetables to the rice instead of the freshly prepared vegetables.

Egg Fried Rice with Seven-spice Beef

Beef fillet is used in this recipe as it is very suitable
for quick cooking and has a wonderful flavor.

Serves 4

INGREDIENTS

1 cup long grain white rice	2 tbsp tomato ketchup	3–4 medium carrots, diced
2¹/₂ cups water	1 tbsp Thai seven-spice seasoning	1 cup frozen peas
12 ounces beef fillet	2 tbsp peanut oil	2 eggs, beaten
2 tbsp soy sauce	1 onion, diced	2 tbsp cold water

1 Rinse the rice under cold running water, then drain thoroughly. Place the rice in a saucepan with 2¹/₂ cups of water, bring to a boil, cover, and simmer for 12 minutes. Turn the cooked rice out onto a tray and set aside to cool.

2 Using a sharp knife, thinly slice the beef.

3 Mix together the soy sauce, tomato ketchup, and Thai seven-spice seasoning. Spoon this mixture over the beef and toss well to coat evenly.

4 Heat the peanut oil in a large preheated wok.

5 Add the beef to the wok and stir-fry for 3–4 minutes.

6 Add the onion, carrots, and peas to the wok and stir-fry for a further 2–3 minutes.

7 Add the cooked rice to the wok and stir to combine.

8 Lightly beat the eggs with 2 tablespoons of cold water. Drizzle the egg mixture over the rice and stir-fry for 3–4 minutes,

or until the rice is heated through and the egg has set.

9 Transfer to a warm serving bowl and serve immediately.

VARIATION

You can use pork tenderloin or chicken instead of the beef, if desired.

Stir-Fried Rice with Chinese Sausage

*This is a very quick rice dish as it uses precooked rice. It is therefore ideal
when time is short or for a quick lunchtime dish.*

Serves 4

INGREDIENTS

12 ounces Chinese sausage
2 tbsp sunflower oil
2 tbsp soy sauce
1 onion, sliced

1–2 medium carrots, cut into
  thin sticks
1$\frac{1}{4}$ cups peas
$\frac{3}{4}$ cup canned pineapple
  cubes, drained

1$\frac{3}{4}$ cups cooked long grain rice
1 egg, beaten
1 tbsp chopped fresh parsley

1 Using a sharp knife, thinly slice the Chinese sausage.

2 Heat the sunflower oil in a large preheated wok.

3 Add the sausage to the wok and stir-fry for 5 minutes.

4 Stir in the soy sauce and allow to bubble for about 2–3 minutes, or until syrupy.

5 Add the onion, carrots, peas, and pineapple to the wok and stir-fry for a further 3 minutes.

6 Add the cooked rice to the ingredients in the wok and stir-fry for 2–3 minutes, or until the rice is thoroughly heated through.

7 Drizzle the beaten egg over the top of the rice and cook, tossing the ingredients in the wok, until the egg sets.

8 Transfer the stir-fried rice to a large, warm serving bowl and scatter with plenty of chopped fresh parsley. Serve immediately.

COOK'S TIP

Cook extra rice and freeze it in preparation for some of the other rice dishes included in this book, as it saves time and enables a meal to be prepared in minutes.

Chinese Risotto

*Risotto is a creamy Italian dish made with arborio or risotto rice.
This Chinese version is simply delicious!*

Serves 4

INGREDIENTS

2 tbsp peanut oil
1 onion, sliced
2 cloves garlic, crushed
1 tsp Chinese five-spice powder

8 ounces Chinese sausage, sliced
3–4 medium carrots, diced
1 green bell pepper, seeded and diced
1^1/$_3$ cups risotto rice

1^3/$_4$ cups vegetable or chicken stock
1 tbsp fresh chives, snipped

1 Heat the peanut oil in a large preheated wok.

2 Add the onion, garlic, and Chinese five-spice powder to the wok and stir-fry for 1 minute.

3 Add the Chinese sausage, carrots, and green bell pepper to the wok and stir to combine.

4 Stir in the risotto rice and cook for 1 minute.

5 Gradually add the stock, a little at a time, stirring constantly until the liquid has

been completely absorbed and the rice grains are tender.

6 Stir the snipped fresh chives into the wok with the last of the stock.

7 Transfer the Chinese risotto to warm serving bowls and serve immediately.

COOK'S TIP

Chinese sausage is highly flavored and is made from chopped pork fat, pork meat, and spices.

VARIATION

Use a spicy Portuguese sausage if Chinese sausage is unavailable.

Crab Congee

This is a typical Chinese breakfast dish, but it would probably not go down too well at a Western table at this time of day! However, it would be welcomed as a lunch or supper dish as it tastes delicious!

Serves 4

INGREDIENTS

1 cup short grain rice
$6^{1}/_{4}$ cups fish stock
$^{1}/_{2}$ tsp salt

$3^{1}/_{2}$ ounces Chinese sausage,
   thinly sliced
8 ounces white crab meat

6 scallions, sliced
2 tbsp chopped cilantro

1 Place the short grain rice in a large preheated wok.

2 Add the fish stock to the wok and bring to a boil. Reduce the heat, then simmer gently for 1 hour, stirring the mixture from time to time.

3 Add the salt, Chinese sausage, crab meat, scallions, and cilantro to the mixture in the wok and heat through for about 5 minutes.

4 Add a little more water if the congee "porridge" is too thick.

5 Transfer the crab congee to warm serving bowls and serve immediately.

COOK'S TIP

Always buy the freshest possible crab meat; fresh is best, although frozen or canned will work for this recipe. The delicate, sweet flavor of crab diminishes quickly: this is why many Chinese cooks make a point of buying live crabs. In the West, crabs are almost always sold ready-cooked. The crab should feel heavy for its size, and when it is shaken, there should be no sound of water inside.

COOK'S TIP

Short grain rice absorbs liquid more slowly than long grain rice and therefore gives a different textured dish. A risotto rice, such as arborio, would also be ideal for this recipe.

Chicken Chow Mein

No noodle section of an Asian cookbook would be complete without a Chow Mein recipe. This classic dish requires no introduction, as it is already a favorite among most Chinese food-eaters.

Serves 4

INGREDIENTS

9 ounces medium egg noodles
2 tbsp sunflower oil
9¹/₂ ounces cooked chicken
   breasts, shredded
1 clove garlic, finely chopped

1 red bell pepper, seeded and
   thinly sliced
3¹/₂ ounces shiitake mushrooms,
   sliced
6 scallions, sliced

¹/₂ cup bean sprouts
3 tbsp soy sauce
1 tbsp sesame oil

1 Place the egg noodles in a large bowl or dish and break them up slightly.

2 Pour enough boiling water over the noodles to cover and let stand while you are preparing the other ingredients.

3 Heat the sunflower oil in a large preheated wok.

4 Add the shredded chicken, finely chopped garlic, bell pepper slices, mushrooms, scallions, and bean sprouts to the wok and stir-fry for about 5 minutes.

5 Drain the noodles thoroughly. Add the noodles to the wok, toss well, and stir-fry for a further 5 minutes.

6 Drizzle the soy sauce and sesame oil over the chow mein and toss until well combined.

7 Transfer the chicken chow mein to warm serving bowls and serve immediately.

VARIATION

You can make the chow mein with a selection of vegetables for a vegetarian dish, if desired.

Egg Noodles with Chicken & Oyster Sauce

The chicken and noodles are cooked and then a flavored egg mixture is tossed into the dish to coat the noodles and meat in this delicious recipe.

Serves 4

INGREDIENTS

9 ounces egg noodles	2 tbsp peanut oil	3tbsp oyster sauce
1 pound chicken thighs	3½ ounces carrots, sliced	2 eggs
		3 tbsp cold water

1 Place the egg noodles in a large bowl or dish. Pour enough boiling water over the noodles to cover and let stand for 10 minutes.

2 Meanwhile, remove the skin from the chicken thighs. Cut the chicken flesh into small pieces, using a sharp knife.

3 Heat the peanut oil in a large preheated wok.

4 Add the pieces of chicken and the carrot slices to the wok and stir-fry the mixture for about 5 minutes.

5 Drain the noodles thoroughly. Add the noodles to the wok and stir-fry for a further 2–3 minutes, or until the noodles are heated through.

6 Beat together the oyster sauce, eggs and 3 tablespoons of cold water. Drizzle the mixture over the noodles and stir-fry for a further 2–3 minutes, or until the eggs set. Transfer to warm serving bowls and serve hot.

VARIATION

Flavor the eggs with soy sauce or hoisin sauce as an alternative to the oyster sauce, if wished.

Ginger Chili Beef with Crispy Noodles

Crispy noodles are terrific and may also be served on their own as a side dish, sprinkled with sugar and salt. Here they are complemented by the gingered chili beef.

Serves 4

INGREDIENTS

8 ounces medium egg noodles	1 red chili, seeded and very finely chopped	2 tbsp lime marmalade
12 ounces beef fillet	$3^1/_2$ ounces carrots, cut into	2 tbsp soy sauce
2 tbsp sunflower oil	thin sticks	oil, for frying
1 tsp ground ginger	6 scallions, sliced	
1 clove garlic, crushed		

1 Place the noodles in a large dish or bowl. Pour over enough boiling water to cover the noodles and let stand for about 10 minutes while you stir-fry the rest of the ingredients.

2 Using a sharp knife, thinly slice the beef.

3 Heat the sunflower oil in a large preheated wok.

4 Add the beef and ginger to the wok and stir-fry for about 5 minutes.

5 Add the garlic, chili, carrots, and scallions to the wok and stir-fry for a further 2–3 minutes.

6 Add the lime marmalade and soy sauce to the wok and allow to bubble for 2 minutes. Remove the chili beef and ginger mixture, set aside, and keep warm.

7 Heat the oil for frying in the wok.

8 Drain the noodles thoroughly and pat dry with absorbent paper towels. Carefully lower the noodles into the hot oil and cook for 2–3 minutes, or until crispy. Drain the noodles on absorbent paper towels.

9 Divide the noodles between 4 serving plates and top with the chili beef and ginger mixture. Serve immediately.

VARIATION

Use pork or chicken instead of the beef, if desired.

Twice-cooked Lamb with Noodles

*Here lamb is first boiled and then fried with soy sauce, oyster sauce, and spinach,
and finally tossed with noodles for a richly flavored dish.*

Serves 4

INGREDIENTS

9 ounces egg noodles
1 pound lamb loin fillet, thinly sliced
2 tbsp soy sauce

2 tbsp sunflower oil
2 cloves garlic, crushed
1 tbsp sugar

2 tbsp oyster sauce
6 ounces baby spinach

1 Place the egg noodles in a
large bowl and cover with
boiling water. Let soak for about
10 minutes.

2 Bring a large saucepan of
water to a boil. Add the lamb
and cook for 5 minutes. Drain
thoroughly.

3 Place the slices of lamb in a
bowl and mix with the soy
sauce and 1 tablespoon of the
sunflower oil.

4 Heat the remaining
sunflower oil in a large
preheated wok.

5 Add the marinated lamb and
garlic to the wok and stir-fry
for about 5 minutes, or until just
beginning to brown.

6 Add the sugar and oyster
sauce to the wok and stir
to combine.

7 Drain the noodles thoroughly.
Add the noodles to the wok
and stir-fry for a further 5 minutes.

8 Add the spinach to the wok
and cook for 1 minute, or
until the leaves just wilt. Transfer
the lamb and noodles to serving
bowls and serve hot.

COOK'S TIP

*If using dried noodles, follow the
instructions on the packet, as they
require less soaking.*

Singapore-style Shrimp Noodles

Singapore noodles are a classic dish and can be served as a main meal or as an accompaniment. This dish combines meat, vegetables, shrimp, and noodles in a curried coconut sauce.

Serves 4

INGREDIENTS

9 ounces thin rice noodles

4 tbsp peanut oil

2 cloves garlic, crushed

2 red chilies, seeded and very finely chopped

1 tsp grated fresh ginger root

2 tbsp Madras curry paste

2 tbsp rice wine vinegar

1 tbsp sugar

8 ounces cooked ham, finely shredded

$1^{1}/_{4}$ cups canned water chestnuts, drained and sliced

$1^{1}/_{4}$ cups mushrooms, sliced

1 cup peas

1 red bell pepper, seeded and thinly sliced

$3^{1}/_{2}$ ounces peeled shrimp

2 large eggs

4 tbsp coconut milk

$^{1}/_{4}$ cup shredded coconut

2 tbsp chopped fresh cilantro

1 Place the rice noodles in a large bowl, cover with boiling water, and let soak for about 10 minutes. Drain the noodles thoroughly, then toss them with 2 tablespoons of peanut oil.

2 Heat the remaining peanut oil in a large preheated wok. Add the garlic, chilies, ginger, curry paste, wine vinegar, and sugar to the wok and stir-fry for 1 minute.

3 Add the ham, water chestnuts, mushrooms, peas, and red bell pepper to the wok and stir-fry for 5 minutes.

4 Add the noodles and shrimps to the wok and stir-fry for 2 minutes.

5 Beat together the eggs and coconut milk. Drizzle the mixture into the wok and stir-fry until the egg sets.

6 Add the shredded coconut and chopped cilantro to the wok and toss to combine. Transfer the noodles to warm serving dishes and serve immediately.

VARIATION

Egg noodles may be used instead of rice noodles, if desired.

Sweet & Sour Noodles

This is a delicious Thai dish which combines sweet and sour flavors with the addition of egg, rice noodles, large shrimp, and vegetables for a real treat.

Serves 4

INGREDIENTS

3 tbsp fish sauce
2 tbsp distilled white vinegar
2 tbsp palm sugar or brown sugar
2 tbsp tomato paste
2 tbsp sunflower oil

3 cloves garlic, crushed
12 ounces rice noodles, soaked in boiling water for 5 minutes
8 scallions, sliced
1 cup grated carrot

$^2/_3$ cup bean sprouts
2 eggs, beaten
8 ounces peeled jumbo shrimp
$^1/_2$ cup chopped peanuts
1 tsp chili flakes, to garnish

1 Mix together the fish sauce, vinegar, sugar, and tomato paste in a small bowl. Set aside until required.

2 Heat the sunflower oil in a large preheated wok.

3 Add the garlic to the wok and stir-fry for 30 seconds.

4 Drain the noodles thoroughly and add them to the wok, together with the fish sauce and tomato paste mixture. Mix well to combine.

5 Add the scallions, carrot, and bean sprouts to the mixture in the wok and stir-fry for 2–3 minutes.

6 Move the contents of the wok to one side, add the beaten eggs to the empty part of the wok, and cook until the egg sets. Add the noodles, shrimp, and peanuts to the wok and toss together until well combined.

7 Transfer to warm serving dishes and garnish with chili flakes. Serve hot.

COOK'S TIP

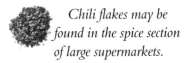

Chili flakes may be found in the spice section of large supermarkets.

Noodles with Chili & Shrimp

*This is a simple dish to prepare and is packed with flavor,
making it an ideal choice for special occasions.*

Serves 4

INGREDIENTS

9 ounces thin glass noodles

2 tbsp sunflower oil

1 onion, sliced

2 red chilies, seeded and very
   finely chopped

4 lime leaves, thinly shredded

1 tbsp fresh cilantro

2 tbsp palm sugar or brown sugar

2 tbsp fish sauce

1 pound raw jumbo shrimp, peeled

1 Place the noodles in a large bowl. Pour over enough boiling water to cover the noodles and let stand for 5 minutes. Drain the noodles thoroughly.

2 Heat the sunflower oil in a large preheated wok.

3 Add the onion, chilies, and lime leaves to the wok and stir-fry for 1 minute.

4 Add the cilantro, palm or brown sugar, fish sauce, and jumbo shrimp to the wok and continue stir-frying for about 2 minutes, or until the shrimp turn pink.

5 Add the drained noodles to the wok, toss to mix well, and stir-fry for 1–2 minutes, or until heated through.

6 Transfer to warm serving bowls and serve immediately.

COOK'S TIP

Fish sauce is an essential staple throughout Thailand. You will usually find this labelled as nam pla.

COOK'S TIP

If you cannot buy raw jumbo shrimp, use cooked shrimp instead and cook them with the noodles for 1 minute only, just to heat through.

Stir-Fried Cod & Mango with Noodles

Fish and fruit are tossed with a trio of bell peppers in this spicy dish served with noodles for a quick, healthy meal.

Serves 4

INGREDIENTS

9 ounces egg noodles
1 pound skinless cod fillet
1 tbsp paprika
2 tbsp sunflower oil
1 red onion, sliced

1 orange bell pepper, seeded and sliced
1 green bell pepper, seeded and sliced
1 cup baby corn cobs, halved
1 mango, sliced

$^{1}/_{2}$ cup bean sprouts
2 tbsp tomato ketchup
2 tbsp soy sauce
2 tbsp medium sherry
1 tsp cornstarch

1 Place the egg noodles in a large bowl and cover with boiling water. Let stand for about 10 minutes.

2 Rinse the cod fillet and pat dry with absorbent paper towels. Using a sharp knife, cut the cod flesh into thin strips.

3 Place the cod in a large bowl Add the paprika and toss well to combine.

4 Heat the sunflower oil in a large preheated wok.

5 Add the onion, bell peppers, and baby corn cobs to the wok and stir-fry for about 5 minutes.

6 Add the cod to the wok, together with the mango, and stir-fry for a further 2–3 minutes, or until the fish is tender.

7 Add the bean sprouts to the wok and toss well to combine.

8 Mix together the tomato ketchup, soy sauce , sherry, and cornstarch. Add the mixture to

the wok and cook, stirring occasionally, until the juices have thickened slightly.

9 Drain the noodles thoroughly and transfer to serving bowls. Transfer the cod and mango stir-fry to separate serving bowls and serve immediately.

VARIATION

Use other white fish, such as monkfish or haddock, instead of the cod, if desired.

Japanese Noodles with Spicy Vegetables

*These noodles are highly spiced with chili and flavored
with sesame seeds for a nutty taste which is a true delight.*

Serves 4

INGREDIENTS

1 pound fresh Japanese noodles
1 tbsp sesame oil
1 tbsp sesame seeds
1 tbsp sunflower oil

1 red onion, sliced
3½ ounces snow peas
1–2 medium carrots, thinly sliced
12 ounces white cabbage, shredded

3 tbsp sweet chili sauce
2 scallions, sliced,
  to garnish

1 Bring a large saucepan of water to a boil. Add the Japanese noodles to the pan, bring back to a boil, and cook for about 2–3 minutes. Drain the noodles thoroughly.

2 Toss the noodles with the sesame oil and sesame seeds.

3 Heat the sunflower oil in a large preheated wok.

4 Add the onion slices, snow peas, carrot slices, and shredded cabbage to the wok and stir-fry for about 5 minutes.

5 Add the sweet chili sauce to the wok and cook, stirring occasionally, for a further 2 minutes.

6 Add the sesame noodles to the wok, toss well to combine, and heat through for a further 2–3 minutes. (You may wish to serve the noodles separately, so transfer them to serving bowls.)

7 Transfer the Japanese noodles and spicy vegetables to warm serving bowls and garnish with sliced scallions. Serve the noodles immediately.

COOK'S TIP

If fresh Japanese noodles are difficult to get hold of, use dried rice noodles or thin egg noodles instead.

Stir-Fried Rice Noodles with Green Beans & Coconut Sauce

These rice noodles and vegetables are tossed in a crunchy peanut and chili sauce for a quick satay-flavored recipe.

Serves 4

INGREDIENTS

10 ounces rice sticks (wide, flat rice noodles)
3 tbsp peanut oil
2 cloves garlic, crushed
2 shallots, sliced

$1^1/_2$ cups green beans, sliced
$3^3/_4$ ounces cherry tomatoes, halved
1 tsp chili flakes
4 tbsp crunchy peanut butter
$^2/_3$ cup coconut milk

1 tbsp tomato paste
sliced scallions,
   to garnish

1 Place the rice sticks in a large bowl and pour over enough boiling water to cover. Let stand for 10 minutes.

2 Heat the peanut oil in a large preheated wok.

3 Add the garlic and shallots to the wok and stir-fry for 1 minute.

4 Drain the rice sticks thoroughly.

5 Add the green beans and drained noodles to the wok and stir-fry for 5 minutes.

6 Add the cherry tomatoes to the wok and mix well.

7 Mix together the chili flakes, peanut butter, coconut milk, and tomato paste.

8 Pour the chili mixture over the noodles, toss well to combine, and heat through.

9 Transfer the mixture to warm serving dishes and garnish with scallion slices. Serve immediately.

VARIATION

Add slices of chicken or beef to the recipe and stir-fry with the beans and noodles in step 5 for a more substantial main meal.

Noodle & Mango Salad

*Fruit combines well with the peanut dressing, bell peppers,
and chili in this delicious hot salad.*

Serves 4

INGREDIENTS

9 ounces thread egg noodles
2 tbsp peanut oil
4 shallots, sliced
2 cloves garlic, crushed
1 red chili, seeded and sliced

1 red bell pepper, seeded and sliced
1 green bell pepper, seeded and sliced
1 ripe mango, sliced into thin strips
$^1/_4$ cup salted peanuts, chopped
4 tbsp peanut butter

$^1/_3$ cup coconut milk
1 tbsp tomato paste

1 Place the egg noodles in a large dish or bowl. Pour over enough boiling water to cover the noodles and let stand for 10 minutes.

2 Heat the peanut oil in a large preheated wok.

3 Add the shallots, garlic, chili, and bell pepper slices to the wok and stir-fry for 2–3 minutes.

4 Drain the egg noodles thoroughly.

5 Add the drained noodles and mango slices to the wok and heat through for about 2 minutes.

6 Transfer the noodle and mango salad to warm serving dishes and scatter with chopped peanuts.

7 Mix together the peanut butter, coconut milk, and tomato paste until well combined and then spoon over the noodle salad as a dressing. Serve immediately.

COOK'S TIP

If wished, gently heat the peanut dressing before pouring over the noodle salad.

Index

Index compiled by Hilary Bird.